SILENT FOR TOO LONG

Emma Sue Miller

PublishAmerica
Baltimore

ISBN: 978-1-61582-891-3
PUBLISHED BY PUBLISHAMERICA, LLLP
www.publishamerica.com
Baltimore

Printed in the United States of America

PROLOGUE

Dear Reader;

Abuse is a tragedy of monumental proportions to those unfortunate to be stuck in its all encompassing grasp. I say 'all encompassing,' because abuse comes in many forms.

Its scope is larger than one individual. Physical, emotional, and mental, it involves not only the one being abused, whether it is women, men, or children, abuse affects whole families, even whole communities.

Ask yourself: "how does it make me feel when I hear of a horrific story of someone being abused in your town, church, school, or maybe right next door? Would I come to the aid of someone if I saw them being hurt by another, or would fear of the unknown cause me to look the other way?

This true story of my own experiences and those of my children will hopefully inspire you to take a good look at this heart rending cycle of abuse and become aware of how far this 'blight,' has spread.

There are things we can all do to help make a difference in other people's lives, whether it is a family member or a complete stranger. Please take to heart my story and the statistics I have provided to better the life of someone else, and yes, possibly even save a life.

I am not going to sugar coat what I have to say. All of us need to know what is happening in the lives of innocent victims all over the globe. It's real and not something that can be shoved under the carpet just to make us all feel better.

I personally put my own children at risk because of the

horrendous abuse I suffered at the hands of their father, I have a lot to answer for, I don't deny this and I will spend the rest of my life making up to my children the fact that I allowed the abuse to continue.

My daughter will tell all in the final chapters of this book please listen to her. If you have children and are in a situation that you don't think you can ever escape from, think again, a child's life is a precious thing, they need nurturing, and love, they need your strength and determination. These facts alone should propel you towards the goal of protecting them from all harm even if that harm may be coming from someone you 'love.'

CHAPTER 1

As a child, my life was wonderful. I was nurtured and protected by the type of parents all children should be blessed to have. Loving and kind, yet ready to administer balanced discipline, never harsh, never unjustified; I respected and loved my parents with all my heart.

Looking back, every single day of my life was good. There were of course times when I would require some type of discipline like all normal children, I always deserved whatever punishment they meted out, which, I'm glad to say was rare.

When I was a young girl I held onto the same dreams as all little girls. I would grow up and marry my Knight in Shining Armor. I would have the most beautiful children and a fairy tale marriage.

If I could have turned the pages of time forward to where I was able to see the nightmare my life would become, maybe I could have done something to change its course, but as we all know that isn't the way it works. Foresight and vision of the future is a difficult thing, but I encourage you all to make sure to always look at the big picture before making any decisions. It may save you a lot of pain and heartache.

Growing up in a small town in a day and age where abuse and dysfunction was almost unheard of I had absolutely no idea that there were families whose quality of life was different from my own. It never entered my mind that there were people who were no better than animals, hunting and preying on the weak.

If someone had told me then, that there were husbands and boyfriends who actually hurt the ones they professed to love, I wouldn't have believed it for a second.

Actually, thinking about it now, animals are much better creatures than the type of person I am going to tell you about.

I was raised to believe that women and children were; to be protected, loved, and nurtured by their parents and mates. I believed this with all my heart, I had the best examples of how to treat one another in a marriage, my own parents!

Of course as you grow, you begin to realize that life isn't all a bed of roses all of the time. Because of my innocence and belief that I would be loved and taken care of by whoever I may eventually marry, I totally missed all of the warning signs.

What warning signs you may ask? Any woman who has survived abuse at the hands of a 'loved one' should already know the answer to that question. As for the rest of you, I hope my story will make it very clear.

There are predators out there that are ready and willing to do whatever it takes to control and hurt the weak. They have no conscience; no remorse, they do all they do to help bolster their own insecurities.

Those of you who know of someone, anyone, whether they be a member of your own family, social group or just a neighbor, who are living in an abusive relationship I hope to enable you to step up and do what you can to protect and help them.

Unfortunately a lot of the time the ultimate price to pay for staying where you are being beaten in one form or another is death.

My high school years were some of the best years of my life; my grades were always above average, I loved to learn, anything and everything but in those days they did not spend time on social issues such as child and spousal abuse. These were problems to be hidden from view; denial was the catch phrase, 'it isn't happening' the lie.

I had goals and dreams like most other girls my age. I wanted to find a career path that would help me continue learning. Back in those days there were many choices to pick from. At that time I chose our family business.

My Grandfather had started a plant nursery as a young man that continued on through the family. My father, mother, brothers, sister, and I all worked together. We all had our areas of expertise and the business thrived.

During my teen age years, I would spend all of my summers at the Nursery working, earning my own money and loving every minute of it. As my graduation from high school got closer I met a man who completely swept me off of my feet.

Greg was a great guy, or so I thought. He was attentive and kind to me. Much older than myself, he had been married before and fought in Viet Nam.

He convinced me that his divorce was his ex-wives fault. Trusting and naïve I believed every word that came out of his mouth. He had fought for our country and I was proud that I had caught the attention of a patriotic Veteran.

My parents appeared to dislike him on sight; I couldn't understand their immediate distrust. They had raised me to have an open mind and to give people a chance and now here they were judging him, I was confused and upset at their behavior. Even though I knew deep down inside of me they would never steer me wrong for any reason, I still felt as if they didn't have my best interests at heart. I was falling for this guy and they were not happy about it.

If I would have just listened to them and took their feelings seriously I would have saved myself much grief and heartache, but I chose not to. Blinded by my own raging emotions, I threw myself into the relationship.

My best friend at that time was dating Greg's best friend who sincerely 'seemed' to be a good guy, so in my newly blooming dysfunction I figured Greg was a good guy too, we were both wrong.

Marie and I had grown up together. Only eight days apart in age we spent our childhood doing everything together. She was the best friend I had ever had and I loved her to death.

Our parents were friends also and spent quite a bit of time socializing together. Marie and I would do the usual goofy things all kids do while our parents were not looking. Like the time we tried cigarettes together in the basement of her parents house. Needless to say, we were both so sick I thought I would throw up a lung; I am still a non-smoker today.

Up to this point I had never been a drinker, alcohol had not held much interest for me. I was busy with my gymnastics and my swim team, my body was my temple and I kept it fit and clean. I had no idea that the subtle manipulations of Greg would forever change that for me.

I was still in high school when I met him and he was a drinker. He drank everyday, all day but he never seemed to be affected by the alcohols effects. I now know that is the sign of an alcoholic but I was seventeen, I had absolutely no idea that he was addicted to booze.

It looked fun and all of my friends drank at their parties so I began to drink a little. A beer here, a sip off of his whiskey there, I had absolutely no idea the horrible effects that his drinking was having on him, so I began to drink every time we were together.

I'll never forget the very first time I was mistreated by him. We had gone to a party on a lake. It was a beautiful day with not a cloud in the sky, warm breezes blowing off of the still water of the lake kept the day at a perfect temperature.

The house that the party was held at was an old, rustic, cabin. I can still see it in my minds eye as if it was yesterday. It was built out of logs and had a porch the size of my own house. There were flowers blooming all over the yard and with the sun reflecting off of the water it held the promise of being a wonderful day.

That 'beautiful and idyllic day marked the beginning of a hellish future for me; with seemingly no way out. My outlook on life and people in general would forever take a turn towards the dark side of human nature. My happy, innocent nature took a serious blow that day. If I could go back and change the events unfolding at that party I would do it in a heartbeat; isn't hindsight a bitch?

It was the first time I had ever drunk alcohol in the hot sun and boy was I in for it. When I felt the very first effects of the mixture of whiskey and the hot day sneaking up on me I began to panic a little.

Up to this point I had been very careful not to over indulge. I knew from my upbringing that drunkenness was not a good thing. I wanted to follow the example of my parents and just have a good time without getting filthy drunk.

When my vision began to blur and I saw two of everything I asked Greg to take me home. I needed to get out of there and be alone. I was scared and ashamed. But he refused, even going so far as to laugh at me.

When I began to cry it was like throwing gasoline on a fire, he got so angry that I felt myself trying to shrink into a place in my mind where I couldn't hear his harsh words.

He informed me that I was embarrassing him in front of his friends and that I should just; "shut the hell up and go sit somewhere." That's the last thing I remember.

I couldn't believe it when I woke up the next morning in my own bed. I had no idea how I'd gotten home or how I had gotten into my bed. I was sick to my stomach and my head felt like a snare drum was pounding its way through the very core of my brain.

On top of the hangover I was worried sick that my parents had seen me arriving home drunk. I loved them so much that I never, ever, wanted to see them hurt because of my actions. But I knew without a shadow of a doubt; my getting drunk was going to hurt and upset them.

As I was on my way to the kitchen to get a glass of water to quench the raging thirst and horrible taste that was winding it's way around my tongue, I had to veer into the bathroom to bow down to the porcelain god. Then, without looking at myself in the mirror above the sink and with my humiliation at an all time high I once again began my trek into the kitchen for my water.

I'd almost made it to the entryway to the kitchen just to run into my mother sitting at the dining room table. She had a newspaper up to her face and as I froze in the doorway she slowly lowered the paper and said, "Your father was up when you got home last night."

That was all she said. She put the paper back up and ignored me. Silently, afraid to speak in case I gave away anything that had happened the night before I got my drink and retreated back into the bathroom for another round of nausea, shame following me all of the way.

When I felt that I had thrown up all that I could, I went to the sink to wash my face and try to make myself look presentable. As I looked into the mirror at my sunken eyes and pale skin I saw a bruise just forming on my cheekbone and a burn on my chin.

I had no memory of what had caused my injuries so I just chalked it up to my overindulgence and stupidity. I would learn later that day that Greg had caused my injuries.

When Greg called me that day, he sounded concerned and worried; "Are you alright?" He asked me. "You fell down, I tried to save you from being hurt but you just slipped out of my hands, I think you may have hit your face on a rock."

"I fell horrible," I told him, "I have a bruise and a burn on my face and I don't remember anything at all, so that's what happened," I was glad to know how I had gotten hurt but at the same time I was unhappy because I knew that it must have been my own fault.

Little did I know that later that day I would get a phone call from Marie who would tell me she had seen Greg hit me in the face. She told me that he was angry that I wanted him to drive me home when he was having a great time. When I had started to cry it made him so angry that he lashed out at me and with his hand balled up into a fist had drove it straight into my face.

This was the first fight I had ever had with Marie. We had been best friends from birth, seventeen fun years together and I informed her in no uncertain terms that I did not believe her. She was hurt but not angry, she told me she loved me and would be there for me if I ever needed her.

I had never—ever—raised my voice to Marie. We never fought, we were best friends in the truest sense. Neither of us had ever gotten so angry at the other that we had to fight or raise our voices, we had way too much respect for each others opinions and right to think and feel however we wanted.

If I had any type of brain function at that time I would have known something was wrong, just the fact that I had gotten so angry at Marie and not listened to her words should have told me that she was right and I was wrong. But I chose ignorance.

Fooled as I was by Greg I hung up on her and spent the day in my room feeling sorry for myself and wishing that he would call me again so I could tell him what Marie had told me.

This was the beginning of my dysfunction and the end of my innocence.

CHAPTER 2

After my high school graduation Greg and I spent more and more time together. For a couple of months I didn't see the side of him that he showed at the party. I believed that it must have either been my fault and had done something to deserve what he had done to me. Or else he didn't do it at all and Marie was wrong.

I opted to believe the easiest explanation; Greg was innocent and I was guilty. When that thought had become firmly established in my mind I began my trip down 'It's my fault lane.'

I feel the need to explain here my true personality, the one I had been born with not the one that was formed during my time with Greg. I want you to be able to see how abuse can literally change your whole outlook on life and even your personality. Abuse is so invasive it went so far as to completely change who I was; changing me into a person who demanded no respect.

Greg had beaten me into someone who was; weak, mentally and physically. I was ignorant of what and who I was becoming. I also became a person who I totally despised, I hated myself, the spineless sheep being led around by Greg.

I was no shrinking violet; I was out going although a little weak physically, five foot four and skinny; but what I lacked for in strength and size I made up for with a strong will and a strong sense of justice. I knew right from wrong and this made me able to stand up for myself and not let anyone push me around.

For the first time in my life I felt as if I was losing a grip on my own personality, but I couldn't quite put my finger on what the problem was. I knew that I was not a very good girlfriend. For one thing I would go and do things with my friends without him and that as I found out was one thing that he would not put up with. I was putting my friendships before my relationship with him. He acted hurt that I didn't 'want to spend time with him,' sulking and sad I let his emotions get the better of me and eventually cut off all ties with anyone who I had up to this point called my friend.

"How selfish of me, how could I love my friends more than I loved him?" He would drill this into my head until I finally gave up all of my other relationships and lived my life exclusively for him.

I now know that this is a tactic used by predatory humans to isolate and control the weak. They are very good at making you think you're a horrible person for putting other people first before their needs and wants. The guilt you feel eventually erodes away any balanced and normal thinking and throws you into a cesspool of guilt and shame. The result is the predator isolates and gains complete control over the weak. That is exactly what happened to me.

I actually thought for years; I was wrong to have any friends at all, my first priority had to be Greg and my marriage. I wasted a lot of years on this type of thinking. I ruined all of my friendships for him; because I truly thought I was the bad one and whatever abuse he meted out to me; I must deserve.

As my eighteenth birthday approached I had become completely entrenched in our relationship. I'd met his mother and sister by this time and his sister Tessa, talked me into moving out of my parents home and into a house with her.

I had never really considered moving out on my own. I wanted to save money and do something good with my life. But against my better judgment, which unfortunately was becoming the norm for me, I agreed and we moved into a house together.

After we had gotten all of our belongings moved in we decided to have a house warming party. There were a lot of people attending, mostly Tessa's friends since mine had all but disappeared out of my life, and we had a keg of beer and some munchies.

Greg of course was at the party and all seemed to be fine until I made the 'mistake,' of taking the keys away from some of our guests who were obviously way too drunk to get behind the wheel of a car. I got blankets and pillows and told them all to stay put for the night or get other rides home because I wasn't going to be responsible for anyone getting hurt on the road.

I thought I was being a good friend by putting their safety first and the safety of others on the roads.

Greg was humiliated by my 'treatment of his friends,' and began to yell at me in front of the whole party. His sister instead of standing up for me and my decision walked away without looking back as he continued to rant at me.

"How dare you embarrass me in front of everyone, who do you think you are? You're an idiot, give the keys back right now!" He yelled an inch from my face.

I was stunned and confused. 'How on earth could he be mad at me for doing something to protect the lives of the people who he claimed to be his friends.' I asked myself over and over but to no avail, I had no good answer for such a question, I was too easily manipulated by then and to prevent myself from being yelled at any further I gave in and gave the keys to Greg.

With a big fat smile aimed in my way he returned the keys and sent all of the guests on their way. The next day we found out that one of the young men at the party had wrapped his car around a tree and was in serious condition in the hospital. Somehow this was blamed on me by Greg, I still to this day do not understand how he could blame me, but blame me he did. He was so good at his mental manipulations he convinced me that the injuries sustained by the party guest was my entire fault.

I was so confused and angry that I decided to confront Greg about what had happened. What he did next was so traumatic that I should have left him right then and there, but I didn't; famous last words?

As I was talking and explaining to him how upset I was, without any warning; he lashed out and brutally shoved me down onto the hard kitchen floor; knocking the wind out of me and bruising not only my dignity but my backside as well.

As I struggled to get up he hit me full on in the face with his clenched fist, believe me when I say he didn't hold back either.

Through the tears and the stars that were now weaving their way across my vision I saw him coming at me again. Somehow I got back up onto my own two feet and ran, I almost made it to the front entry door before he caught up with me.

Grabbing a handful of my long hair he yanked me to a violent halt, "Don't you ever run from me again you worthless bitch," he screamed at me.

With his hand still wound tightly in my hair he threw me to the ground managing to tear a handful of hair straight out of my skull. The pain was excruciating, I had never felt anything like it in my life. I had been raised in a peaceful happy home, not a violent, stressful home. This type of violence was alien to me, I had no idea what to do or how to stop the assault.

Over and over again the blows fell, on my face, my legs, anywhere that he could get a blow in he did. It seemed as if time had stood still and the vicious hits would never stop. When the pain became unbearable he stopped suddenly and leaned down to gaze silently gaze into my eyes as if he was assessing the damage and what else he could do to me.

His face was so close to mine that I could see every single little vein in the whites of his eyes. What I saw reflected there scared the hell out of me, I didn't see only violence, I saw hatred. I had never in my quiet life ever seen a look such as the one Greg threw at me that night.

His eyes drilled into mine without wavering and in their depths was something sick. He actually looked happy to be able to serve out some 'punishment,' on me. His face was purple by this time with huge veins pulsating in his neck and forehead. I was petrified to the point where I froze like a rabbit trapped by a wolf, I remember wondering, "If I don't move maybe he will spare my life."

He saw my confusion and fear and smiled. I don't know how to describe what he looked like at this point. I could have sworn he was changing into someone or something else. Like a demon having its fun; his delight at hurting me showed on his face, I felt myself drawn into his eyes; I saw my own murder there by the hand of someone who had sworn to love me. This realization gave me a momentary burst of strength and I kicked out as hard as I could.

He was so busy feeling proud of himself for beating down someone much weaker than himself that he was off of his guard. I saw this and kicked out as he was leaning over me. My foot found its mark and landed squarely in his chest knocking him backwards.

Scrambling like a crab I managed to get myself up off of the floor. We were between the kitchen and the front hallway with the front door to freedom a mere few feet from me.

I had been a gymnast in high school and was very limber and very quick but unfortunately I was not quick enough. When I felt his hand grab hold of my hair once again I knew I was done for but it was still early enough in our relationship where I tried to fight back. I wasn't completely dysfunctional yet.

Kicking and biting I fought for my life but he was way too strong for me, he trapped me in the corner of the front door and the hall closet with no where to run.

With a snort of something like amusement he proceeded to kick and hit me over and over again. First he would aim for my face and then he would kick me wherever he could, my legs, my stomach, my back, it didn't matter to him. He appeared to be having fun and that was when I decided to once again try to fight my way out of the house to safety.

I struggled to keep my wits about me, my head was becoming foggy from the fist he had smashed into my face over and over again. I was wobbly on my feet but I was not going to give up yet. I could still see out of one eye, so gauging the distance to the door I waited for him to pause in his cruel assault. When the time came I once again kicked out as hard as I could; landing a glancing blow on his leg and ran.

I suppose I must have surprised him since he had beaten me so severely that I looked as if I couldn't have ran if I wanted to, he hesitated long enough for me to swing open the door and run into the dark, cold, night.

I saw a light on in a neighbors house so I headed that way rehearsing the whole way what I would tell the people who lived there. I was embarrassed and ashamed again so I decided to lie. I would tell them my phone was out and I fell into the ditch on the way over to ask if I could borrow theirs.

I was dysfunctional enough by this time that I couldn't see how stupid that sounded. I never for one instant thought they wouldn't believe my story. I hadn't seen myself yet and didn't know the extent of my injuries. If I could have seen the mess that was left of my face I may have changed my plan but at this point I didn't know I looked like an accident victim.

So I stuck to my plan and approached the house slowly all the while trying to regain some semblance of control over my hurt and raging emotions. I stood on the neighbor's doorstep for a few seconds more. I actually had started to feel guilty. Looking back now I wish somebody would have shook some sense into me. But you know when you reach a certain point in your diseased way of thinking there is really nothing anyone can do or say to you to make you understand that you are being used and taken advantage of and it is wrong.

I told my story to the older couple who answered the door. It was obvious they didn't believe my story and asked if they should call the police. I was so ashamed by what had happened I told them no, my brother would pick me up and I would be fine.

This is a good point for me to try to make my readers understand that even when an abuse victim tells you they are fine and they do not need help from the police or from anyone else it is a total lie.

They do need help and they do need the police, they are unable to think logically anymore because of the fear that resides deep inside of them. If that sweet couple would have ignored my protests and called the police I truly feel I would have come back to my senses and got the help I needed to get away from Greg and the violence.

I do not blame them for not doing so, we lived in a time where interference was not the norm, but there is no excuse today. We are an educated society who needs to step up and help those weaker than ourselves.

19

I didn't know at that time my face was black and blue from my chin all the way up to my forehead. Both eyes were black and swollen with a myriad of cuts crisscrossing the planes of my face. There was blood running from my nose and one ear, I must have looked like a bombing victim to them.

They tried to reason with me but I wouldn't listen to them, I just wanted to be left alone to lick my wounds in private. When the woman of the house hugged me I almost broke down again, but I rallied against the desire and walked out of their house to wait for my brother.

When I saw Johns Jeep coming up the road I felt so relieved I hobbled out to meet him. I had no idea of the condition my face was in. John took one look at me and without saying a single word ran to the house where Greg was hiding like the coward he was and did everything he could to get inside. Greg had the house secured to the point where John couldn't get in. It was probably a good thing that he couldn't gain access to Greg because I truly believe my brother may have killed him.

That should have been my breaking point and I should have completely cut off any relationship with Greg, but I was firmly entrenched in my unbalanced and poisoned way of thinking by then and of course I didn't.

I couldn't see the damage I was causing in my own family. Just the fact my brother had to come out late at night and rescue me from Greg should have made me realize I was doing a great injustice to John.

Why I didn't is still a mystery to me, it is completely out of character for me to act the way I was. What if he had gained access to Greg and killed him? That would have been my fault and I would have had to live with the guilt for the rest of my life. Thankfully that is not what happened but think about it; what if it did?

My brother and I were very close. I loved him and yet I was so used to the way Greg had taken over my mind that I didn't see the hurt I was causing the ones who truly did love me, my own family. I was willing to watch my brother do whatever he wanted to do to Greg.

I was selfishly heaping unnecessary stress onto my family and they had done nothing wrong to deserve it. There's that hindsight again; looking back now makes me physically sick.

It was within my power to stop the horrible nightmare I had been living and protect my family from the hurt I was causing them. Yet, I didn't do anything to make that happen. I continued to believe that 'Greg hurt me because I had done something bad to deserve it.' I felt as if I did not deserve to be saved from him, I was bad and that was that.

We rode in silence all of the way to my brothers house. When we arrived he turned to me and said, "I don't know what is going on with you and Greg but you can stay with us for as long as you need to. There is always a place in our home for you, you know that don't you?"

His loving words were like a hot poker being shoved into my cold heart, I say cold, because I now know that I had turned off any of my emotions that may have caused me more hurt than I had already experienced. I couldn't allow myself to feel, it would have made my life even more traumatic.

So, for years I disappeared into a life that was a sham and a lie. Hiding myself behind a wall of self pity and depression I turned my back on anyone who might make me 'feel again.'

Remember, by this point you 'know that it is your fault you're being hurt by the one you love.' You will do practically anything to keep yourself from being beaten again. With every blow from his fist a piece of me was broken away. Like a sculptor chipping away the flaws from his creation; the abuser does what he needs to do to chip away anything that may give his creation originality or may deviate from how he sees the finished statue.

The next day when I got out of bed I went and took a good look at myself. I couldn't believe what the mirror was showing me. I didn't even recognize the woman looking back at me through the slits where my eyes were barely peeking out from. I had pain in every inch of my body.

As I stood there looking at what had become of me I tried to tell myself that I would never let that happen to me again. So, armed with a tentative strength, which at that time I found out I obviously didn't possess, I tried to form a plan of what I would do next.

I knew I didn't want my parents to see me or to even know what had befallen their daughter, it would have broken their hearts and upset them needlessly so I decided to hide myself at my brothers house for however long it would take to heal up.

My sister-in-law was so kind to me. After helping me dress my injuries she sat me down and told me about her own family's problems with abuse. Her father was a drinker and he would hit her mother regularly.

She told me that for years she thought that was the normal way for families to act. If you deserved a licking you got one. Unfortunately the licking was when he was drunk and for no good reason at all. After meeting our family she told me she knew her family was dysfunctional.

Her mother had stayed with her abusing husband with the result; he had tried to kill her mother with a gun and when that failed he turned the gun on himself and blew his brains all over their house. My sister-in-law had to witness the act and help to clean it up. When he felt as if he was losing control and power over his wife he took his own life.

Whereas I thought; growing up with a loving happy family was the norm, she had grown up in an abusive family and thought that was the norm. It was a lesson that I once again should have taken to heart and cut the ties to Greg immediately. But when he showed up at my brother's house and begged me to forgive him; I'm embarrassed to say I did forgive him and I did go back to him.

When he promised me he would never, ever hurt me again I believed him. I found myself justifying his behavior by blaming myself. For what? I honestly can't tell you. He beat me for the simple fact that he wanted to and he could. I allowed it and he knew it.

He had me so completely under his evil control that my thoughts were in a constant jumble. I would think to myself after every incident; "its okay, I must have done something to deserve this so I should forgive him and go back.' Against the wishes of my brother and sister-in-law I returned to my house and the monster named Greg.

CHAPTER 3

When Greg decided to move in with us his sister moved out. She was angry at his assumption that he could just move right in without asking first. Which was fine with me, she had proven herself to not be the type of friend that I wanted anyway. She could have stopped him from hurting me but she chose to turn a blind eye.

Sadly I've discovered through the years; there are a lot of people who will not go out of their way to help someone in my situation, they would much rather live their uneventful little lives wearing blinders and ignoring anything that may upset them. 'It's not my problem or my fight,' the path of least resistance is usually the way most humans walk.

Today, if I saw a woman being abused by her 'loved one,' I know I would interfere and say anything I could to make it stop. I would not stand for it and I would make sure that I did everything within my power to help the one being abused.

It kills me inside to know there are women and children out there who are, right now, going through what I went through. Many of these women feel they have no recourse but to stay with the abuser, but dear reader that is as far from the truth as you can get.

But I digress

Time continued on for a couple of months with no big blow ups or any more violence from Greg and we settled into a life of sorts. I worked long hour's everyday and was tired all of the time and if Greg chose to ignore me for a while that suited me just fine. Up to this point I thought I was in love, little did I know that emotion I was calling love was really fear.

Greg had a son from another marriage who we had the joy of seeing on the weekends. He was a good boy, quiet and sweet I quickly came to love him as if he was my own.

When his father was gone during the day, we spent those hours doing things together. He was a sensitive little boy and I spent most of the time he was with us doing what I could to buffer the horrible way Greg treated him.

Greg would go out of his way to berate him constantly, the negative way he would talk to his son made me sick. He was only four years old at that time and unable to process the way Greg would discipline him. He began to turn into himself when he was at our house rarely doing anything that might draw any attention to him, in order to protect him from the way his father would treat him.

David was a teeth grinder, Greg blamed him for that saying he was keeping everybody awake with the noise. He would actually get up in the night to wake David up to spank him. If he accidentally dropped something or made noise at an 'inappropriate time,' he was sent to his room or spanked.

I'm not saying those of you who administer balanced discipline to your children should not use spanking as a form of punishment. I did not use spanking on my own children because of the violence I suffered, it would have broken my heart to raise my hand against my child. I chose other non-invasive means to punish such as; time out, or chores. These methods worked quite well for me without any corporal punishment.

But when I say he was spanked by Greg I am actually saying he was brutalized by his father. I did what I could to defend David but Greg would of course wait until we were alone later and inform me: "David is my son, how dare you try to tell me how to parent him. The boy needs discipline," (the boy seemed to be the only name Greg would ever use to address his son), "you don't know anything about raising kids, you're too stupid to know what to do. So how the hell can you tell me how to parent my own son?"

Usually these tirades included him punching me where he knew there would be no bruises, he was becoming very good at using violence without leaving any visible marks. Then if I tried to tell anyone what was happening to me I wouldn't have any outward signs of being brutalized.

He would tell me to mind my own business, 'David was his son, and he would administer what discipline, 'the boy,' would deserve. He reminded me over and over again that I was not a mother and if I ever became one I would suck at it.

"How dumb can you be?" He would say, "You don't know anything, your just a dumb little blonde who can't do anything right, ever!"

His little barbs always hit their mark, my heart. I believed I was stupid to think I could raise a little boy. I had never had kids and hadn't had the privilege of being around them much. "He was right," I would tell myself over and over again: "You are stupid."

Yet I couldn't help myself, every time we had David I still did everything I could to protect him from his father. He was an innocent; no four year old deserves the type of mental abuse his father would heap on his poor little psyche. He was a wonderful child and I still love him to this day. I am honored to be a part of his life.

He hasn't seen his father for many years and that's the way David wants it to stay. I need to let you know why David chose to stop coming to our house.

When he was ten years old Greg told David that his mother was a whore and he was not his son. He forced that poor kid to under go DNA testing so that he could prove his claims and stop paying child support for him, which he rarely did anyway. Surprise, surprise, David was his son and he was stuck paying child support.

David's mother and I had a relationship of sorts. Being the new wife I was uncomfortable around her until I actually got to know her. She told me stories of her life with Greg and encouraged me to leave him as soon as possible. She tried and tried to convince me that I was in danger; I chose ignorance and stayed with him.

Even after everything he had done to me and to his own son I stayed. Why? You might ask, because I was well and truly engulfed in my illness. Abuse has a way of over-powering your thought processes and you cannot make the right decision. I don't know how else to describe this to you.

I constantly told myself I was stupid, lazy, ugly, etc. I believed every single word that my brain threw at me. I was being sucked into a chasm of dysfunction and I truly felt as if there was no hope for me. I sometimes would sit and wait for death. I willed it to over take me and give me the peace I so desperately needed.

Of course it never happened. I still woke up in hell every morning. I thought if I willed myself to die that it would eventually happen. I didn't want to ever wake up again. Life was just a necessary evil and I wanted out. But I didn't have the guts to use suicide as my avenue to freedom.

I discovered later as my mind healed and I was able to be my own person again that I was not a suicidal type of personality. I had people in my life that at that time I thought did not love me anymore because I was with Greg. Deep down I still knew that they would have been devastated at my death.

I knew that suicide was the ultimate form of selfishness and I just couldn't do that do the people who cared about me.

Can you imagine being a child and knowing that your parent didn't want you anymore? How could a child process that type of information? Us as parents have to love, teach, and nurture our children; protecting them from all harm no matter what form the danger may take.

CHAPTER 4

One hot summer day there came a knocking on the door. It was a couple, a man and a woman who told Greg they were preaching door to door to help people to learn the good news about God.

He invited them in and told me to go to my room and stay there while he visited with them. I didn't want to go to my room like a child, so with a defiance rarely shown by me I held my ground and stayed.

Oh boy did this make him mad but he couldn't do anything about his anger or he would show these strangers his true colors. He turned his back to me and began to talk to the missionaries.

Up to this point in my life I had never been religious. The only exposure I had to religion was when my parents would send us to Sunday school. I didn't take the church seriously since my parents would drop us off with money for the collection plate and go back home.

Marie and I figured that if they didn't go then why should we. Instead of going into the church we would wait for our parents to drive away and go off into the town to spend our collection plate money on candy. When it was time to be picked up we would be waiting.

The couple began to talk about the bible and offered us a free home bible study. They began to talk about the scriptures and some of the things they were saying were strange to me.

They said there was no hellfire, Jesus did not die on a cross, and women must be in subjection to their husbands and the men in the congregation. That last concept, that men were over women sent a bad feeling through me but seemed to excite Greg.

They said they would come once a week and teach us the bible. When Greg told them I would accept the offer and they could come every week to study with me I was appalled. I didn't want to study the bible I wanted them to use their free home bible study to help make Greg a better person, if that was even possible.

Before I knew it I was scheduled for a home bible study every single week. I realize now that this religion appealed to Greg because he felt that his abuse of me would go unnoticed because men ran the congregation. This unfortunately for years was true. The 'Elders' managed to get him out of two DUI'S, now you tell me who on earth would do that for anyone?

Carol came once a week, sometimes alone and sometimes with other members of their church. Every time she came to the house to conduct my bible study she always put a scarf on her head. When the study was over she would remove it. When I asked about this she told me that; 'a woman is not allowed to teach or preside over the congregation. They must show their subjection to the men and to 'God,' by covering their head.

Okay, I thought, this is a little frightening but I had to keep silent in case Greg overheard me saying anything negative to Carol. I would have had hell to pay if he for one minute thought I was going to fight against having this study. He had found another avenue to control me with and there was no way he was going to let that slip out of his fingers.

Up to this point in my 'friendship,' with Carol, I'd kept silent about the horror I suffered at Greg's hands. My brother was the only other human who knew what I was going through and when I had stupidly left his house to return to Greg, I had sworn him to secrecy. As far as I knew he had kept my secret and unfortunately his distance. I didn't blame him, it was my entire fault.

There was a tentative trust growing between Carol and myself, even though I still had my walls up to stop anyone from knowing anything about me, I needed to talk to someone. The emotional pain

I was feeling every day felt like a huge ball of twisted nails and glass. I needed an outlet and I hoped talking to Carol would be that much needed release.

After I had made the decision to trust Carol to keep my confidences, I actually, for once, looked forward to my bible study that week. Thankfully she was alone when she arrived, I wouldn't' have been able to talk to her with any witnesses, I was so ashamed of my life that it would have been humiliating for anyone else to know.

I waited silently for her to put on her 'head covering,' and to say a prayer for our study. I hoped that there was truly a loving god who would, through these people, help me find safety and peace.

It had been a long time since I had cried, I was dead inside to those types of emotions, and there was no way I could give into tears until the words began to tumble from my mouth.

Once started I told her everything, from the beatings to the way he treated his own son, the whole time I spoke and cried, Carol sat quietly with absolutely no emotion on her face.

I explained to her that I felt as if the violence I endured at the hands of my boyfriend was in some way my fault, but I wasn't totally convinced I really did deserve what was happening to me.

I still had some of my common sense intact and was smart enough to question whether I really did deserve everything that Greg did to me. I hoped Carol would be able to help me to see reason and give me answers to those unspoken questions all abuse victims have.

*Is it truly my fault this is happening?

*What did I do to deserve this?

*Am I a horrible person who doesn't deserve to be treated with respect?

*Am I really such a bad person?

When I came to the end of my story Carol was still sitting silently with a dead pan look on her face. When I observed this look alarm bells started to sound in my head and I grew quiet, afraid that this possible source of help was actually going to be no help at all.

Without a word she took out her bible and began to look up scriptures. Every single scripture she read to me was about how a woman must be in subjection to her husband.

Greg and I were not married at this time and she focused on this fact. The scriptures she read to me all seemed to put me in the place of the bad guy and Greg in the spot of the good guy.

She informed me that 'god' would not help me unless we remedied the situation that we were living in. We had to be married and then 'god' would be able to step in and help me.

Greg and I had never discussed marriage unless he was telling me what a rotten wife I would be. When she read these few scriptures to me I felt a cold chill come over me and I knew I was sunk. I was an idiot to trust Carol and I knew without a doubt that I was doomed to stay with Greg forever. There would be no help coming from her, I knew this and felt the icy fingers of fear creeping into my mind.

She was going to tell Greg I'd told her all of our dirty little secrets, how I knew this I don't know, but I was right. Carol went to her husband who went to the elders of the church who then went to Greg and told him what I had said.

Greg was forcing me to go to all of the church meetings which were five a week. One evening maybe a week after I had confided all to Carol the elders came up to us after the meeting and asked to speak to us, the look the two elders of the congregation gave me was cold and strange.

'Here it comes,' I thought. I was right to worry about Carol breaking my confidence. I discovered there were no secrets among the people of the church, gossip and judging was rife and I was going to be stuck smack dab in the middle of it. But, that is not what worried me, I have never cared what people think of me, I worried about what was going to happen to me when we got home.

We all met in the 'back room,' and the elders proceeded to tell Greg everything I had told Carol. As they spoke Greg glanced at me and what I saw in his eyes caused me to feel more fear than I had ever felt before.

Outwardly he was calm and even agreeable. He told the elders that we had a small fight and I always tended to 'blow things all out of proportion.' He sat with a meekness I had never seen in him before as the older men of the congregation 'counseled us.'

That counseling consisted of scriptures explaining the roles of men and women in a relationship, but since we were not married these really wouldn't apply to us until we actually, 'did the right thing,' and got married.

Greg convinced them I was emotionally unstable and told them he would make sure everything was okay. He would talk to me and fix the problems that had erupted in our relationship.

The elders seemed relieved that he was going to take a hold of the reins of our life and make sure all would be well. They ended our little meeting on that note and left us to talk alone in the 'back room.'

Greg said nothing to me, he gave me the look I had seen earlier, the one that said, 'you're sooooo going to get it.' He got up and exited the room leaving me there to stew. He knew I was afraid and it fed him with some insane type of satisfaction. This was not going to be a good night for me.

The drive home was silent, neither one of us spoke, we were both lost inside of our own thoughts, mine thoughts of pain and fear, his of power and hate.

When Greg pulled into the drive way he reached across the front seat of the car pinning me back into the seat with his fore arm. He turned a face full of spite and disgust my way and smiled. I looked at him and knew I might die this time.

I couldn't get myself to care if he killed me or not. I didn't want to live and since I was not able to take my own life I figured I would let him take it for me. I had nothing to live for. I knew I had ruined any future we may have had together because I was such a bad girlfriend. I deserved what he was going to do to me and I really didn't care anymore. The woman I used to be was gone now; replaced by a weak, spineless, and stupid person.

He slowly removed his arm; he seemed confused by my lack of reaction. I exited the car and walked slowly into the house trying to delay the inevitable. The very minute the front door shut behind us his hand was in my hair. He loved to grab me by the hair, it left no marks but hurt like hell.

"How dare you lie about me," he screamed a mere inch from my face. His hot breathe and spit engulfing me. "I didn't do anything to you that you didn't deserve. You asked for me to discipline you by acting like a stupid bitch."

By this time he was pulling me around by my hair towards the hallway that led to our bedroom. The whole way he ranted and screamed abuses at me, horrible things said to cause me as much pain as possible. His words used to be like a knife carving out a piece of my very soul, but tonight I didn't care. He could say anything to me he wanted; I was as cold inside as a grave and had no fight left in me. The lack of sympathy and caring from Carol and the 'elders,' had hit me so hard I just let myself go dead, 'nobody cares,' was the foremost thought in my mind.

"You seem to think you have it so bad here, I guess I had better make sure that comes true for you then." He continued to yell, over and over again, saying things meant to hurt and capable of destroying any strength I may have left.

When he reached the door into the bedroom some of my old fight rose to the surface and I began to struggle some, not a lot yet but enough to excite his lust for inflicting pain. He liked it when I fought back, it made him feel powerful, so I tried not to show any fear but when he violently tore my shirt off I knew it was fight or submit.

I grabbed for the door jamb to stop his forward momentum but I was not strong enough and he prevailed. Over and over again he called me names, horrible names I couldn't even say out loud but he seemed to have no problem with it, all the while kicking me in the stomach, back, and ribs.

This wasn't the first time he had raped me and wouldn't be the last. The only thing I could do was lie still and take it. Going limp under the monster I tried to leave my body and my mind to go to a place of refuge, somewhere I wouldn't feel the pain. I had discovered quite accidentally during a beating that I could leave my mind and think about other things to protect myself from the mental trauma of his assault.

Flying through the sky like a bird I would retreat into happy thoughts. I thought about being a little girl again and being wrapped in the warm safety of my fathers arms where I would never be hurt again.

When it was over I got into the shower and tried to scrub away the feel and smell of the rape. Soap and water may be able to wash away the physical trauma but not the mental. Every time I closed my eyes I could still see the hate and disgust on his face just before he attacked.

No matter how hard I scrubbed I still felt dirty. I washed my skin to the point where it would turn red but the stink of his evil still clung to me and made me physically sick. I vomited and vomited until I couldn't vomit anymore.

After every beating, Greg would disappear for hours and then reappear drunk and sorry. But this particular night he did not leave, instead he took out his bible and began to read to me. He told me that I needed God's guidance because I was such a bad person.

Somehow, the scriptures he would read to me made me look like a horrible wife and him a wonderful husband. I was astounded at the way he could twist and turn the words that were supposed to give hope and balanced advice into a guilt trip that made everything my fault.

Somehow the church elders had convinced him that we were living 'in sin,' and that was a situation that must be rectified immediately. The elder's opinion of Greg was all important to him so Greg told me we would be married, where we would be married and when. I had no desire to get married, especially to him, but I did it anyway. I didn't have much fight left in me; I chose the path of least resistance and went along with him to save myself from at least one beating for disobedience.

I felt as if I had no other recourse. I had successfully put myself in a situation where I could see no light at the end of the tunnel. In my sick mind I figured it was either I marry Greg or I go crawling back to my family and risk being lectured and told how stupid I was. Of course that was exactly what I needed, but at this point in my life I didn't see it that way.

I already got that treatment from Greg and the thought of my family reminding me of how the mess I was in was my own fault made me so sad that I couldn't go home. I now know that my conscience had become diseased and didn't work the way it was supposed to, instead of telling me when something was morally wrong it told me lies and fabrications created from my own insecurities. This breakdown in my conscience allowed me to justify everything that happened to me with unbalanced lies and deceit.

My family would have lovingly helped me to get away from Greg and become normal once more. They would have been there for me. But my conscience convinced me that I would heap unnecessary hurt on my parents and that was something I was not willing to do. I still kick myself for believing this to be true.

My wedding day was not a happy day for me. I was sick to my stomach through the whole ceremony, which of course was in our house so Greg could keep control over everything that happened.

My grandmother had been so wonderful to me through the process of planning the wedding. She had absolutely no idea of the nightmare I was living in; I made damn sure of that. She did everything she could to help me. That alone should have told me that I could have turned to my family for the help I so desperately needed.

A church elder married us and that was that. I had to go along with him; I didn't want to give Greg any reason to beat me. He still would give me little slaps and push me around; he really enjoyed doing that to me. Back then I knew I must have deserved it so I kept my mouth shut and decided to never try to talk to anybody ever again, besides; nobody would believe me anyway.

I was truly alone in my nightmare. How I had gotten to this point I couldn't really fathom. I was afraid of Greg; that was how he controlled me.

The people I could have gone to for help all thought I was okay. I smiled at all the right times and said the right things; I got very good at faking that all was well. My life was by now snowballing into a huge ball of dysfunction and stress. It was gaining momentum daily as it rolled on and on with time; gathering everything bad into its coldness.

The one time I had tried to get help from the people in the congregation who claimed to serve 'god,' I was read scriptures and married. Then I was beaten and raped by Greg. I knew if the people who claimed to be servants of god wouldn't listen to me, then nobody would.

I lived in a self imposed loneliness. I was so completely embarrassed and ashamed by the abuse I shut my mouth and just took it. I found out later there were people in my life that would have done everything they could to save me from the monster who was my husband.

But when you are in an abusive relationship and determined to hide your humiliation at what's happening to you there never seems to be a safe way out. He was so good at beating me down in everyway I was emotionally unable to focus and think clearly.

I had mastered the art of fakery. The instant my feet entered the church my smile was set and I was ready to start my act.

I made sure no one would see the real me, the lonely, hurting woman whose day was sure to end in either violence or all engulfing sadness.

It was the same in all aspects of my life. Work, business, social events, my doppelganger was at the fore always. I would not allow anyone to see my true life, my misery.

With continued abuse your powers of reason become foggy. The mental beatings combined with the pain and humiliation of every single kick and punch forces your true self and mind back into a dark, locked, cell.

I was truly under his control, weak and pathetic I had no self-respect, yet, little did I know I was strong, stronger than I could ever imagine, I had the strength to overcome any obstacle, even Greg.

From that time on Greg would force me to sit in the most uncomfortable chair we owned and read scriptures to me nightly. He didn't just read the bible to me he carefully chose the scriptures he would share with me. Taking them completely out of context he read only the ones that would be useful in manipulating and controlling me.

Sometimes he would read scriptures about the coming end of the world. "Armageddon is right around the corner," he told me. He loved to try to make me fear the coming holocaust against all disobedient humans on the earth. I guess he thought I would be more susceptible to his mental abuse if I thought I would die by 'god's' hand because I was a bad person.

I never believed for a second that 'god' was going to come roaring down in a fiery burning war chariot to destroy all the wicked. As far as I was concerned, that would be the act of an evil entity; not one who had sworn to love and take care of his human creations. If I was insane enough to argue with him this point he would hit me and berate me.

I actually tried to pray to the god of the bible; but nothing ever changed, the abuse continued and I was beaten into submission by his fanaticism. That was my last hope; prayer; I prayed constantly day and night but nothing ever happened. I resigned myself to being a member of the church; at least, I figured maybe he wouldn't hurt me as often.

CHAPTER 5

Three months after we were married I became pregnant with my daughter. I was sicker than I'd ever been in my entire life. Three months of nausea and exhaustion. During those three months I was ridiculed and slapped because I was unable to do the house work like I used to.

Taught by my mother I was an excellent house keeper and was proud to keep my house clean, but as sick as I'd been it became extremely hard to keep up with all of the work. I still worked full time at the nursery and between my job and the house work I found myself exhausted.

I struggled with the cooking during my morning sickness, which in all actuality was day and night sickness. My doctor tried to convince me to be admitted to the hospital to make sure the baby was going to be okay but Greg would not allow it. I couldn't be that far from his evil grip. No way would he let that happen.

When I became pregnant I was one hundred and ten pounds, by the end of those three months I weighed in at ninety two pounds. This of course was my fault also. He blamed me for not eating on purpose. The doctor tried everything he could to convince Greg to admit me to the hospital but he refused. He said he could take care of me better at home.

Greg became so incensed with the doctor I thought he was going to physically assault him. I could see the turmoil in my doctor's eyes as Greg pulled me across the waiting room. I tried to meet the doctors eyes, I needed him to see the turmoil and fear there; I stupidly thought if he could read the message there he might help me.

I was wrong. He lowered his eyes to the floor and said nothing as Greg aggressively pulled me from the office. I could expect no help from this professional or from 'god,' I was now truly alone.

Do you know how it feels to have everyone turn their backs on you? I do! I makes you feel hollow inside, like something left to die in the hot sun after getting smashed by a fast moving car. You know that every car that passes can see your agony but they just continue on by, averting their eyes so as not to have to go out of their way. Your insides twist up into a hot knot of depression.

I felt so alone I began to think of taking my life again. But of course I was carrying a precious life and I would do everything I could to protect my baby. I now had a new fear on top of all of the other nightmares I lived in.

My doctor was the only one I could afford at the time; because Greg had refused to ever let me go back to see him I lived with the thought of having no help to have my baby. I worried I would have to have her alone at home. Thankfully I was able to enroll in a teaching hospital. I had to let interns poke and prod me but that was okay; I was going to have the help I needed to give birth.

During my pregnancy my life was a living hell. Greg didn't allow weakness of any kind. If I was ill or in pain he would tell me to toughen up, 'do you know how many women have to have their babies out in the wild with no help whatsoever?' He would ask me while I was throwing up my breakfast.

He enjoyed telling me of the women in Viet Nam who would give birth in the rice paddies and then go right back to work with their babies on their backs. Good for them I say, but that was not what I had in mind for my birth. Of course I couldn't voice this to him but I didn't care about those women in the rice paddies I cared about getting the best care for my baby.

During my pregnancy the women of the congregation tried to come by and give me some help and advice since this was my first child. It made Greg so mad that someone other than himself was in 'his house' taking care of 'his wife' that he put a stop to any visitors. I don't know what he told people but all of a sudden they stopped coming by. He succeeded in running off anyone who may have helped me in anyway. He was afraid of being found out for the brute he truly was.

Abusers will do whatever it takes to isolate their victim and ensure they are completely reliant on them for everything. The only people he allowed near me was his mother and his sister. Of course they knew Greg was a monster but they were silent on the subject. Another avenue of possible help that was taken away from me, they were loyal to Greg and obviously didn't care about me.

I guess in their own way they tried to be good to me, they both tried to help me as much as Greg would allow.

During the first few months I was carrying my baby Greg still hit me. Although he was careful not to hit me in the stomach, it caused me much anguish to think my baby may be injured by its father. I tried to 'be good' so that I would spare the baby any violence but that was a waste of my time, he didn't let up on me even during pregnancy.

The emotional trauma that I endured during those long nine months was horrible. He stopped hitting me when I began to 'show,' but he just replaced it with even more emotional abuse. He continually told me, 'I was going to be a bad mother, and that I was an idiot to think I could raise a child. He would tell me he wanted to take the baby when it was born and just leave me to wallow in my own stupidity.'

He could never carry out that threat because the church would not allow divorce or separation except on the grounds of adultery. It didn't matter that he would beat me and abuse me in any way he could think of, oh no, unless one of us committed an adulterous act we were stuck with each other.

Like I said before; his reputation in the congregation meant everything to him and he wasn't about to do anything to ruin that. I was too weak to do anything other than just go along with him and the laws of the church, I thought I was stuck and so I just rolled over and did what I was told by my husband and the men running the congregation.

When I went into labor it was snowing outside. I'll never forget that because snow used to be such a joy to me. It brought up all sorts of happy memories from my childhood. As I looked out the window at the falling white flakes I felt nothing but an all consuming fear.

Fear of the unknown, fear of being beaten, fear of anyone finding out what was happening to me, fear of dying, fear was my constant companion. It caused me not to be able to eat or think straight. It also kept me from doing anything to help myself.

Fear can be a healthy emotion. For example; when you are thinking of doing something potentially dangerous, fear can help you to analyze what you're planning to do and help you to make the wise decision in whatever course you may be planning. It can also stop you from rushing into a bad situation.

The fear I carried with me was destructive and over whelming. It's like poison to your insides as it wraps it's evil tentacles around your whole psyche. You hurt deep in the core of your very being all of the time. It causes physical illnesses and pain, which in my case caused stomach ulcers and an insane weight loss.

I was spending the day at my mother-in-laws house when my water broke. I had no idea where Greg was but his mother finally tracked him down at a local bar. He had made it a habit to drink as much and as often as he could. When she found him he was extremely put out that I had to go into labor when he was having a good time with his buddies.

When he finally arrived at the house he was so drunk that he began to yell at me, "You're timing, as usual, is bad, I was having a good time with my buddies and you decide to stick your stupid little nose into my fun and have 'your' baby tonight. You stupid bitch," with that said he reached out and grabbed my arm and began to man handle me into the car.

As we drove away towards the hospital I sat in silence, enduring the painful contractions and staring at the bruises just beginning to form on my wrist. The visible reminder of how much I was despised and hated made my heart sink; I didn't think I would ever feel happy or loved again.

When we arrived, the nurses saw that I was distressed and asked if I was sick or if the pain was too much, I lied and told them, 'yes,' it was much easier to just agree with whatever they said than to tell them the truth.

I was in labor for only a few hours, but during those couple of hours he never let up on me.

"You're doing your breathing all wrong, your so stupid you can't even remember how to breath correctly." He kept telling me over and over again, like a Chinese water torture it wore away at any strength I may have had to be able to endure my labor.

I had planned on having my baby naturally with no pain medications. I chose this route because I couldn't afford all of the drugs they would use to numb me for the birth. But as his voice continued to cut through my head like a whip without letup, I decided to ask for the pain meds. I couldn't concentrate and knew I had to get rid of either the labor pain or my husband.

As the anesthesiologist was administering the spinal Greg made the mistake of harassing me in front of him, needless to say he was unceremoniously thrown out of the room. The doctor told him that he would not be allowed back in as long as he continued to act the way he was.

Needless to say when we arrived back home with our daughter, I got a good beating. He had been holding back while I was swollen with child but as soon as the baby was no longer in the way he resumed right where he had left off.

He accused me of telling the doctor lies about him, of course I had done no such thing but he was convinced and I had to pay for it. All of you women, who have experienced labor, know you are unable to form a lucid thought even if you wanted to. All you think about is getting the baby out of you.

I had a beautiful, healthy baby girl. She was the only good thing in my life, the light in my dark world. I would do whatever it would take to protect her from her father. Thankfully at that point in our lives he did not abuse the baby. That doesn't mean he wouldn't abuse me in front of her, that seemed to make him happy,

Plus, I think he knew if he laid a hand on my daughter I would get the strength only a mother can possess, take my baby, and leave. That was something he would not allow to happen. I was his property, to do whatever he wanted with. He seemed to crave the control he had over me, like a drug.

CHAPTER 6

During my marriage to Greg I wasn't allowed to spend very much time with my family. My Grandmother who I loved with all of my heart, and who I miss every single day, would call me often. She always seemed to have a way of knowing when I was at the breaking limit, even though she didn't know how I was treated by Greg.

I was happy to spend all of my spare time with my grandparents when I was young. They spoiled me and even though I knew this I never took advantage of them, I had way too much love and respect for them. They loved me in return, the type of love that all grandchildren should receive from their grandpa and grandmas.

When they passed away it took a piece of me with them, and for the first year after they were both gone I would smell Grandma's perfume in the house and dream she would call me on the phone to let me know she was okay.

I told my sister of this one day and was I surprised to hear she had the exact same experiences in her home. She also received phone calls from Grandma in her dreams.

My grandparents would call on a regular basis to invite us out to dinner, of course, Greg would not go, and I was usually not allowed to go either. He would let me go occasionally so as to belie any stories I may tell them about him. He was always trying to cover his bases by using a type of dysfunctional yet diabolical way of thinking.

I have to confess to you; it gets really old trying to constantly come up with 'stories,' or if the truth be told 'lies,' to tell them why I couldn't come to see them. I was still covering up the truth of my life to my family, after months and even years of abuse this becomes the norm and you really get pretty good at conjuring up lies to tell them.

"Liars never prosper," is one of the truest statements ever penned down. Besides what the lies do to chip away at your conscience, you also forge a path of distrust with every single person that you lie to. Eventually after so many lies you begin to forget what you've lied about and the truth slowly begins to leach out.

I've spent many years trying to make up for all of the falsehoods I had to tell to hide what was happening to me. My family has forgiven me but you know; I can't forgive myself. I've come to a sort of resignation to my past, yet when I remember some of the things I told my family, stupid lies, I still feel the shame just as if it happened yesterday.

Today I am a completely different person. Lying is something I cannot do. I've discovered it's much easier to tell the truth and face the consequences immediately; then to string a bunch of tall tales along behind you. Telling the truth eases your stress to a normal level and your life flows much better, because you aren't trying to come up with a new lie to justify the last one.

My grandparents may be gone now, but their memories are held dear in my heart. Even now, as I'm writing this I have to cry over the loss of two of the most important people to have ever been in my life. I hope with all of my heart that those of you who are reading my story will take to heart the fact that you only have one family.

They are your blood and your life, nurture and love them now, don't let anything come between you and those you love. Especially don't let another human do anything to wreck your relationships. I don't care if it is a husband or a wife, to try to come between a person and their loved ones purely out of selfish motives is evil; don't allow it. People come and go in our lives; family is forever.

Still, to this day, my family has no idea of the horrendous acts of violence I endured at Greg's hands. I kept it from them following my 'escape.' It was hard enough to think about and remember the past without shame roaring up to meet my thoughts; to talk about it was something I was not willing to do. I was in and still am to a certain degree in denial.

As time went on it began to dawn on me that one day I would die at the hands of this maniac. I would be alone with him and he would take my life and then bury me in a shallow grave somewhere.

These thoughts didn't upset me; I was half hoping he would put me out of my misery since I didn't seem to be able to do it myself. This diseased way of thinking was the norm for me in those days. I simply didn't care. When he would brutalize me to the point where everything began to hurt I didn't care. After time there were no more tears and no more self pity. It was truly a relief to not be able to feel fear as strongly as I did in the beginning.

Don't get me wrong, I am not telling you this so that you can justify how you are feeling right now, I am telling you this so that you will be able to see this is a poisonous way of thinking. You will never be able to get the strength you need to make informed decisions if you retreat into total denial.

Greg continued to associate with the church and the people who attended it. I had to go to the meetings with him or he would beat me. I didn't discuss my home life with the people in the church. After the one time I had tried to appeal to the woman who was conducting my home bible study and was stabbed in the back by her I knew; there was nothing I could do or say to these people to get help.

It was important to Greg that he was well known and popular with the parishioners. He needed to be accepted and popular with these people. He was an expert at hiding his true nature. It was scary to watch him change from the violent monster I lived with into a completely different person.

The kind, naïve, parishioners had no idea who Greg truly was; a violent, hateful misogynist who loved nothing better than to hurt those weaker than him, especially women.

Whenever there was an issue that arose in the congregation such as; someone needed help or food, he was the first one in line to help them. We never had enough food for the family but he made sure that if someone else needed something he would move heaven and earth to get it for them.

The church had a program where they would go out into communities and build more churches with volunteer labor and materials. Greg was in construction and made sure he was at the forefront of all the activity. This made him look like a great man and he relished the attention.

I never went to these building programs; I couldn't stand to watch the way the other women in the congregation would look at him. They were constantly telling me; 'how lucky I was,' to have such a great husband. He was very good at never showing the evil inside of himself to others. That was reserved solely for me.

I managed to make friends of a sort with some of the women in the church. Even though some of these women seemed like they would lend a listening ear my way, I couldn't let myself put down my guard. They were kind and polite to me at all times, but I can't help but think if they knew what my life was truly like, would they have stepped up to the plate and helped me? In time, I would have the opportunity to test this theory.

CHAPTER 7

After the birth of my second child, a son, I sunk into a deep depression. I went through the motions of living my life and being alive inside when there was nothing further from the truth. Greg had effectively killed every positive emotion I had. All there was left in my heart was the love I felt for my children. They were precious and needed to be protected at all costs, this usually meant more beatings for me, but so be it, I would take them if it meant saving my babies from harm.

By this time Greg had effectively buried any self esteem I may have had left; he'd also buried anything that made me an individual, my free will was cremated by this monster and it's ashes spread out as far as he could hurl them.

Still, thank goodness, he made no effort to abuse the kids physically. After James was born, we moved as far out in the country as he could get us. My family was starting to try to come around again and see the children and myself. Greg didn't like that at all so he moved us far enough away that it would be a little bit of a drive for them to come over to visit.

After we moved, he began to drink more heavily, if that was even possible. I would find bottles of whiskey hidden all over the house along with the most disgusting and degrading pornography I'd ever seen.

Sex to me was a violent and hurtful act designed to degrade and soil a woman. It meant nothing to me. It was just a way for a man to overpower and control women, this is exactly how I thought, and it would take years and a wonderful man to change that for me. When I knew he was going to sexually attack me again I retreated into my; 'happy place,' and I felt nothing.

One of the worst 'punishments,' I'd ever received came about five years after the birth of my son. The reason for this punishment was for nothing more than; my going to the grocery store with the money he had in his wallet and buying food.

It's actually kind of a funny story now that I think of it but at the time I didn't find anything amusing about it at all.

He'd come home the night before drunk and once again; out of control and violent. I was working two jobs at the time and he was drinking the money I made as fast as I could make it. This night he had stayed out until three in the morning much to my relief. The less he was home the better.

I was pregnant with my third child and sick and tired of his violence and his attitude. I was a mouse with no will of my own; all I could do was watch my children go without.

This particular night was pretty much like the rest. I worked all day came home and went through the motions of being alive. After looking in the refrigerator for something to make for dinner I knew by it's emptiness that this would be a lean night. I had made it a habit at dinner time that my children would eat and if there was anything left I ate.

There was enough to feed the kids but once again; I went without. That was okay with me, I happily gave all to my children. I have no regrets for this, children come first.

After putting the kids down for the night I sat in the dark, alone, crying. I rarely shed a tear for that creep but this night was too much for me to bear. I worked my ass off and got nothing for it.

My wages were low, I was a woman in a mans world and getting a raise, even though it was a family business would not happen for me. As a result; the bills were not getting paid and my children were not getting the proper nutrition they needed. This stress was way too much for me and I could feel the panic I lived with on a regular basis begin to rear its ugly head again.

My world was spiraling out of control; I was pregnant again, working full time and not making enough money to pay the bills or buy food. I had to visit the local food banks on a regular basis and when I did get my pay check the first thing I did was buy groceries.

If I didn't spend the money on food right away, Greg would come and take all of it and disappear for the night, coming home at all hours drunk to the point where he couldn't even form a sentence and ready to fight.

I was sitting quietly in the front room, the lights were turned out and my thoughts in their usual turmoil when I heard his truck driving up the rocky driveway. Taking a deep breath I prepared myself for whatever he had in store for me.

I sat quietly in front of the cheery fire, my fear beginning to rise into my chest. It felt as if a ball of stress and fire were spinning their way through my guts. The pain that came with the stress usually made me physically ill but this night I was going to try to control it and not show the fear that was my shadow.

Usually when he arrived home he expected me to be awake and ready to serve him in anyway he saw fit. I froze waiting for the sound of the truck door slamming and his boots stomping up the steps. Funny thing; that didn't happen, all I could hear was the sound of the night and my own heart pounding out its anticipation.

After a few minutes I got up and went to the window to see what he was doing. I couldn't believe my eyes, his truck door stood open and he was nowhere to be seen. 'Oh, oh,' I thought, he was going to sneak up on me and kill me.

I saw him then, he was on the ground crawling like a bug, and it was one of the funniest things I'd seen in a long time. He inched along, drooling like a dog and mumbling to himself, the mud from the recent rain coating his body.

I had to stifle my laughter so he wouldn't hear me; I felt my laughter begin to turn into something else that I couldn't control. It was hysteria; I knew I couldn't let in to the desire to laugh uncontrollably so holding my hand across my mouth I continued to watch as he attempted to haul his drunken body up the steps to the front door.

Somehow he managed to haul himself up the side of the door jam to insert his key into the lock. I held my breath, not moving or making any sounds. I could hear his key going into the lock just to fall out again and again. How he managed to find the lock in the first place was beyond me. Even the fact that he found his key after dropping it in the dark as polluted as he was amazed me.

His heavy breathing was audible through the crack under the door and I waited for the inevitable. Then, there was nothing. I didn't trust my ears; he had fooled me before just to get me to come close enough where he could grab me. This fact helped me to remain silent.

Men like Greg are like a cancer, just when you think it is in remission it rears its ugly head once more and attacks. I hoped against hope that he would just give up and go away, he didn't fulfill this wish; he did the next best thing and passed out cold on the front steps with the rain beginning to fall.

I waited long enough to judge he must be completely unconscious because drunks can fool you, just when you think they can do no more, somehow they rally and start to move again.

After insuring he was well and truly out, I crept out to where he had fallen and went for his wallet, hoping he had saved some of my paycheck. I reasoned he was so drunk he would never remember if he had money or not. Unfortunately for me the next morning he did remember he had money. A lot of it, I didn't know where he could have come up with so much cash but I took it.

I couldn't sleep that night; I waited for him to wake up, the anticipation killing me. Thankfully he stayed put on the front steps. Back in those days there were no twenty four hour stores, I had to wait until the next day when the stores would be open.

The next morning; quiet as a mouse I got the kids up and dressed. When we left the house I carefully lifted both kids over his prostrate body warning them not to say a word. They obeyed me even though their faces showed their fear.

I spent all of the money I had lifted from him. The whole time I was shopping I was worrying about what would happen to me if he found out what I'd done. Any of you who have felt this all invasive inner fear knows how destructive it can be. I had to constantly fake being happy and bought the kids anything they wanted. They deserved it; they had no toys, no food, and no future, all because of me.

On the drive home the kids were ecstatic, I had not only bought them the food they so badly needed, I took them and bought them both brand new clothes, lots of them, shoes, shirts, pants, socks, and underwear. My poor children either had to wear hand me downs or torn up and holey clothes.

Looking at their happy faces now helped me to overcome my aversion to arriving home; I actually felt their father would be happy to see their smiling faces since they rarely smiled at all.

Where we lived was isolated and quiet, we had neighbors who were members of the church but they never visited, Greg didn't encourage visitors, at least not anyone who would want to visit me. He had the men from his congregation stop by on occasion but I was sent to where I couldn't interact with them. This suited me since I had no respect for these men either.

When I drove up our driveway; he was waiting for me, thunderclouds raced across his face and along with these dark threats was anger. I'd lived for a long time with him but I had never seen his face quite like this before.

I tried to ignore my inner voice telling me to turn around and just drive away and continued up the drive. I attempted to park the truck without giving away to the children the kind of mood their father was in but my children had learned in their short little lives what each look on their fathers face meant.

They grew quiet and as soon as I stopped the truck they raced out of there like the bats of hell were behind them leaving me to deal with Greg. I thought I was ready but I didn't count on the fact he was holding a chain saw in his hands.

The minute I opened my door to exit the truck he was there; filling the space with his body. He was eerily quiet and just stared at me with so much evil radiating out of his eyes I knew I was dead.

Out of confusion I guess, I began to babble to him about money and buying food, trying to make light of the situation. I was so nervous I'm sure I didn't make a lot of sense but still; he remained quiet, not saying a word. He just continued staring at me, his eyes boring into mine without wavering.

As the silence lengthened he began to smile a smile of pure malice, and without a word he cranked the chain saw into life. I will never forget the sound and the smell of the vicious weapon as he raised it slowly; his eyes never leaving mine. Its spinning blades were inches from my face; the exhaust, and noise filling the cab of the truck with its menace.

Over his left shoulder I could see the faces of the children watching us out of the dining room window. The look on their faces must have mirrored mine. They were scared and their faces told it all. This realization hit me hard, 'if he kills me what will happen to my babies,' was all I could think.

When the kids had left the truck they'd left the passenger door open. I fumbled with my seatbelt, my trembling fingers trying to release its hold on me. He was close now, taking his time, taunting me, his delight at my panic showing on his face.

I do not know how I accomplished it but I managed to throw myself out of the open door. I must have caught myself on something in my rush to escape and landed in a heap on the ground.

Laying there I could hear the roar of the saw getting closer and closer, but the rain soaked ground was so muddy I couldn't get to my feet. Slipping and sliding I tried to retreat away from him. All I could see in my minds eye was my children and I knew I had to get away this time or else.

As he came around the front of the truck he began to rev the engine of the chain saw to scare me further before he struck. Then; for some strange reason the saw gave a hiccup and fell silent.

This was strange because Greg kept his tools in the best working order that he could. There was no reason for that saw to quit like that, but I didn't care, I had been given a reprieve, so taking advantage of it I managed to get to my feet.

Greg tried and tried to get the saw to kick over for him but to no avail. So with a roar like a wild animal he threw the dead machine at me, barely missing my head. I ducked and once again fell victim to the wet and slippery conditions falling unceremoniously back onto my butt.

I could still see the faces of my two children screaming and crying at the window to the house. Greg had ordered them to stay inside of the house but what they were witnessing was too much for their delicate emotions and they both burst out of the house and began to run for me.

Their tears raged down their cheeks and I knew I had to leave. If I stayed and the kids got in the way they could be killed. I would protect my children and do what I needed to-do to make sure they came to no harm.

With that sentiment firmly entrenched in my head I screamed as loudly as I could. Somehow I made it to my feet and ran, trying to get Greg to follow me and put as much distance between our battle and the children.

This diversion worked and Greg took off after me as I sprinted down the driveway and away from the kids. He was following behind me closely; I could hear his labored breathing and his threats getting closer and closer. Thankfully he was out of shape from his disgusting lifestyle and had to give up the chase.

He stood at the top of the driveway, laughing out loud that I would have to come back sooner or later. He was right of course, what mother could stay away from her children? Up to this point he hadn't hurt the children physically, but if I wasn't there to take the abuse I knew he could turn on them to make them the object of his desire to hurt and punish.

I knew without a shadow of a doubt I was the object of his hatred. Why? I don't know. Even through the horrible way he treated me I remained loyal and did all I could to be a good wife and mother.

Greg was always angry and hateful but he still retained some sort of control over his actions. He was calculating and mean, with every type of 'punishment' meted out to me carefully planned out and executed.

This night he acted as if he was out of control with no thoughts except to hurt and humiliate. I'd rebelled and took his money without his permission. He didn't care if it was for food and clothing for his own babies. No, that never entered his mind. All he could see was I needed to be disciplined and controlled by him. As a result he seemed as if he had no lucid thoughts.

Boy was I wrong. His behavior was nothing more than a ploy orchestrated to put me off my guard so he could get his hands on me. I had completely misjudged him.

It was getting dark by this time and I had been hiding out in the woods for a couple hours. I could still hear the kids crying for me, I had to go back. I discovered later this was his plan all along, he had figured I couldn't stay away; he was right.

Up until now, as I write this; I have never spoken of this incident out loud to anybody. I've tried to purge my mind of this night but to no avail, but as I write this I can already feel all the lingering dysfunction left over from this experience melting away.

As night fell I began to work my way slowly back towards the house. We lived in a one bedroom, broken down, travel trailer that was situated up on a rocky lot. There were so many rocks you couldn't take a step on the property without dislodging or kicking one.

Consequently, every single step I took, no matter how furtive I attempted to be; made noise. I had to take a step and pause, take a step and pause, this was time consuming, but I didn't want to draw any attention to myself.

It was getting darker by the minute but I was no stranger to hiding in the woods. When Greg became too overwhelming for me to handle; I would go to my 'retreat,' in the woods and think. Greg also was very adept at getting around our woods in the dark since he had hunted me down a few times after I'd disappear for a while.

It still came as a surprise to me when I ran smack dab into him. When I felt his body blocking my way and his hands come up to grab my upper arms I knew I was done for.

The perimeter of our property was rocky and hilly. We both stood on the very edge of a narrow path leading to our driveway. Anyone who might have seen us would have thought we were a pair of lovers sharing an embrace. Nothing could have been further from the truth.

I suppose he must have thought it would be great fun to push me down the hill and watch me bounce. Smiling in that sadistic way of his he began to apply pressure to my arms, testing me to see if I would struggle.

When he realized I wasn't going to do anything to fight him he gave a mighty push and down the hill I went. As I tumbled to the bottom I tried to slow my momentum by grabbing onto the green foliage whizzing past. I must have been rolling faster than I thought for as I grabbed hold of the branches they tore right through the tender skin of my hands.

I finished my roll to the bottom of the hill just to lie there dazed and unable to move. Somehow he had beat me down to the bottom and was there waiting for me, with his cowboy boots on he proceeded to kick the hell out of me.

The very first kick will stay with me forever. He aimed for the most vulnerable part of my body; my stomach; and with a mighty swing of his leg drove his pointed toe cowboy boot right into me.

I couldn't believe the pain. He had kicked me before but had not done it for quite a few months and I was totally unprepared for the agony that spread like a wildfire throughout my body. Instinctively I rolled myself into the smallest ball possible in a feeble attempt at protecting myself.

Grunting with satisfaction he continued on, over and over again. Not one part of my body was spared from the onslaught; my head, my torso, my legs, arms, you name it, and he made sure he didn't miss it.

It seemed as if the attack went on for hours, to this day I couldn't tell you how long he brutalized me in those woods that night. But I can tell you that when I began to lose consciousness; I felt a bizarre kind of peace coming over me. After a while you don't feel anything anymore, I knew he was still beating me but I barely felt it.

When Greg realized I was no longer struggling against him he leaned down and whispered to me: "count yourself lucky that this is all I do to you."

With that said he wrapped his hand firmly in my hair and began to drag me behind him up the driveway and towards the house. The last thing I saw was my children watching their father dragging me up the driveway, their little faces a study of confusion and horror.

I thought I heard their cries but I couldn't' be certain of anything at that point. Pulling my head up so that we were eye to eye he said; "you deserve this you worthless bitch," then he let go of my hair and my head fell hard onto a rock and my world turned black.

CHAPTER 8

I woke up slowly; I was disoriented and confused. It was cold and wet and at first I had no idea where I was. Greg had left me lying in the driveway. I had passed out from the pain and blows to my body; I guess it ceased to be fun for him anymore when I didn't move anymore so he just left me lying there, alone and hurt.

The sun was just coming up and it looked to be a sunny day, but not for me. I hadn't gotten the news that I was pregnant again with my third child. Maybe if I knew I was pregnant at the time I would have done more to stop the abuse, I don't know. When you're so deeply entrenched in your disease and dysfunction you don't always make the best or the right decision.

I felt horrible and wasn't able to walk right away. I had to lie there like an animal waiting for my body to respond to my commands to move. I hadn't yet seen the kids both watching me out of the windows of the house. Their father was making them observe 'my punishment,' so they could see how bad a mother I was.

It took some time to be able to get up on my own two feet and approach the house. I was afraid, yes, but my children were in there so that is where I had to go.

I knew I had some major injuries to my body but I had to buck up and work through the pain. It felt as if my jaw might be cracked and some ribs hurt. I was surprised by the lack of broken bones. Come to find out later; after a car crash, my doctor informed me,' I had very small and flexible bones,' that's what saved me.

I count myself lucky; I am one of the ones who survived. I lived to tell my story. There are many, many others who are not so lucky. Their funerals tell it all.

I once again tried to contact the 'elders' of the church. They looked at my bruises and asked me, 'what did you do to provoke this?' I am dead serious! Not one of those men asked me if I was okay. Not one!

On top of their lack of any type of caring they told me my neighbor, who just happened to be one of the elders of their church had heard the assault and did nothing to help me.

In fact, they told me he actually covered his ears with his pillows to muffle the sound of my screaming. I don't remember screaming at all, but I must have been crying bloody murder for them to hear me. Then to not do anything to help was an atrocity in itself.

I will add though, they did try to talk to Greg about what happened. They read him scriptures and he told them he was sorry I was such a bad wife but he would work at making our marriage work.

This is when I realized my spirit had been broken by this monster and I had to do something to survive and escape. There would be no help coming from the church, I was well and truly alone.

When I say my spirit had been broken I mean I no longer cared about anything. Sure I still loved my kids but even then; I was in a place mentally where I couldn't help or protect them. I was useless as a mother and a person. That had to change.

I began to plan that night after my meeting with the elders. It would still take me a couple years and a lot of planning to escape, but escape I would.

It took me many years to see that even though Greg did not physically abuse the children, he was heaping emotional abuse on their tender little minds. Just the fact they had to watch their father beat and hurt their mother, and listen to the things he would say about me, was absolutely abuse.

"Your mother deserves all she gets. She's a bad mother and she needs to know that." On and on he would go without letup, bombarding them with negativity and hate. I have to ask myself today, 'what emotional burdens do my children carry as a direct result of my not getting them away from the abuse sooner?'

The church did not allow the celebration of holidays. Birthdays, Christmas, you name it and they would not celebrate it. Because holidays were steeped in Paganism, we were not allowed to take part in them.

This practice was readily taken up by Greg, by not allowing us to celebrate holidays we would spend less time with my family. That made him extremely happy. It was one more way for him to keep me away from anyone who may care about me. Plus, he would have more money for himself and his filthy habits.

To make a long story short; I was beaten, starved, abused not only physically but mentally and emotionally. I was told I was stupid, ignorant, a whore, a slut, and good for nothing. After being told these things for years over and over again you begin to believe them. I truly believed them to be true.

Now I know that nothing could be further from the truth. I agree that what happened to me was my own fault. If I had the mental fortitude to tell myself that he was an abuser who hid behind his religion to get away with everything that he did and then took the initiative to leave; I would have saved myself and my family a lot of grief.

Women of the world; stand strong and firm, do not allow yourself to be taken advantage of and hurt by the ones who 'claim' to love you. It is wrong and if you allow it you will enable the abuser and hurt every single person who is a part of your world.

Let me say this one more time; you will hurt EVERY SINGLE PERSON who loves you. No one is exempt from the resulting avalanche of dysfunction that results from an abusive relationship. NO ONE!

That fateful night showed me that I was putting my children in harms way because of my emotional and mental death at the hands of their father. Somewhere deep in my psyche I knew I could stop the abuse and get out of harms way, but was I still too sick mentally to do anything about it. Not any more.

Children are the only true innocents on our world. If their own parents can't keep them from harm, then who can?

We were all children at one point in our lives. Can you remember what it felt like when you were hurt or scared? Children are not able to process negative emotions when they are young. They need positive and good reinforcements. They are not able to rationalize what is happening in their family.

Their confusion and fear must overwhelm them to the point where there is deep psychological damage done. When babies are born the bond between them and their mothers is the strongest bond in the entire inhabited universe. They look mainly to their mothers to teach them how to control and balance their emotions. One way they do this is by observing how we as parents act in our everyday lives and in all of our relationships. The things we do and everything we say has a direct impact on them.

It was my undeniable responsibility to insure my children were protected from harm by any type of outside forces. This is easier than trying to protect your children from forces inside of your own family; it is difficult but attainable.

It was this fact that drove me to get my children out of harms way.

CHAPTER 9

When I say I had to plan my escape, I mean just that. You cannot just get up and walk away from an abuser. As a result I stayed and after the birth of my third son I began to plan. There was no way that child would grow up in the same household with his father. I had already kept the other two kids in hell, I wouldn't do it again.

As he grew older and stronger I knew it was time for me to make my move. What ever plan I came up with had to be not only financially feasible, but also had to be safe for all of us. Thankfully my parents offered us a home to rent. Being able to move into an affordable house took care of the first part of my plan.

I jumped at their offer and began a serious plan to finally leave Greg and take my family to safety. I had yet to be able to separate from Greg, so to put him off his guard I had to let him believe we would be moving together. Having to do this wasn't easy, pretending and lying takes a toll on your conscience, even though it was for a good reason.

I figured once in the house together, when he next caused any type of problem; I would be able to use the fact we lived in my parent's house and kick him out. This was sound reasoning at the time. Sadly I neglected to reason out that he may not want to leave. What then?

Even though the house was reasonably priced I still didn't make enough money at my regular job to pay rent and provide food. I needed more income and Greg wasn't any help in that department. He was still drinking his money and mine as quickly as we earned it.

I decided to get a second job; I didn't care in the least that I went without life's necessities, but my kids were suffering from malnutrition and stress and if I had to step up to the plate and make more money, so be it. I began to work the family business during the day and during the night I worked at a restaurant.

Unfortunately I wasn't able to make enough money, even with two jobs, to buy food and necessities and move at the same time. Greg wasn't any help so I made sure the children had their new home and whatever they needed to sustain them. I once again went without. But I did this gladly, seeing the kids getting all they needed was all I wanted.

Through the years I never once, not even for a second, bad mouthed Greg to the children. When he would do some act of abuse or say something horrible, I did not tell them their father was bad; only that what he had done was wrong.

I chose this route because; if I told them their Dad was bad over and over again, as children they would be even more traumatized. I so badly wanted to instill in them what was right and what was wrong.

I would give them the knowledge they would need to make their own decision about their dad. That was my goal and happily I was very successful.

I can't say this strongly enough; mothers: give your children the tools they need to be able to make decisions for themselves. I don't mean decisions about what to wear or what to eat, I mean life's decisions. Give them the information they need so they can look at the world as a whole and make good, balanced judgments. You may save your own daughter from becoming the victim of abuse.

Do not say: "Your father is bad, I hate him." Instead point out what he is doing is wrong and then teach them what is right. This is simple but very powerful. Your children will then be able to make decisions based on the information you provide. It will be their decision; not yours.

Oh sure, I could have called him names and told them what a horrible person he was. I wanted and they needed to be able to make up their own minds about how they felt about their dad. To me that was the right and moral thing to do.

By his own actions; Greg proved to the kids the kind of man he truly was. Some of the things he did to the kids stayed with them and helped them to see the monster inside of their dad.

Greg enjoyed giving gifts to the kids and then taking them away. Remember, they were not allowed to have anything to do with secular holidays. As a result they had very few toys. We lived out in the country so I decided to get the kids each a little kitten.

I'd read that pets can have a profound effect on your health, knowing my children were 'depressed,' I felt the kittens would help them to be able to show more emotion.

Greg waited just long enough for them to bond with their new pets and then informed them, 'you are not taking good care of the cats so we will get rid of them.'

He then made sure enough time went by for them to think about losing their kitties, then took both cats, shoved them into an ice chest, and put it in the back of his truck. He made sure the kids were watching this power play. Yes, I say power play because that is exactly what it was.

How pathetic, a grown man using his own children's emotions to bolster his own sick insecurities, pretty disgusting wouldn't you say?

His hateful behavior didn't end there. He actually made my children get into the back of his truck and sit on the lid of the ice chest while he drove to the middle of the woods.

Once there; he made them both throw their little pets out into the woods, with that done he drove home berating them the whole way about their, 'behavior.'

After this incident the kids got even quieter in his presence. After a while, maybe a few months we had a stray kitten show up at our doorstep. My oldest son immediately bonded with the kitty and I let him keep it. I was determined this time to protect the cat and my son's emotions.

I was firm with Greg about the cat; I tried to reason with him about why pets are so valuable in a household. He 'pretended' to listen and without a word walked away from me.

I actually thought I may have won a round but after a few days I saw this was as far from the truth as possible.

It was a Sunday, the weather was warm, and the air was calm. Greg seemed to be in a good mood, which was rare, so we all seemed to breathe a collective sigh of relief and tried to enjoy the day.

Of course since it was Sunday, he got us all up early and would make us all sit and listen to him read the bible. It was one of those times in the day where I knew I wouldn't get beat. He never beat me on a Sunday.

On our way home later that day from the church meeting Greg seemed to change right before our eyes. This wasn't rare and it sent chilling signals through me. He was planning something and it couldn't be good.

As we drove up the drive way, my son's kitten ran to meet us. My son had named him 'Biffer,' he loved that cat. What happened next was so horrific I can still hear and see the results of that tragedy.

Seeing the little kitten in the yard waiting for us, Greg steered the truck directly at its little furry body and ran it over right in front of all of us. I don't want to describe the results of his evil plan, but needless to say, it traumatized us all.

So you see, by his own actions, Greg ostracized his own children.

CHAPTER 10

The straw that broke the camels back and helped me to make the decision to finally leave Greg happened when my youngest was just turning two years old. We had moved into my parent's house and had been living there for a mere few weeks when I had a visit at my work from a social worker.

She informed me she was from 'Child Protective Services' and that a complaint had been filed against my husband for child molestation. The abuse she told me; wasn't against one of my own children but against a female family member. He was being accused of taking indecent liberties with another member of my family.

As I felt my heart sink I also felt red hot anger rise up into my chest. I knew the allegations were probably true, what they were at that time I had no clue. She didn't divulge any information to me. She said we would be contacted by the State and actions would be taken.

I will not go into the details here in order to protect the life of this person. This relative of mine is completely blameless and innocent; I will protect them by my silence.

Thoughts whirled around in my head like a mini tornado. 'If he was capable of doing what he was being accused of; then was he capable of hurting his own daughter?'

This thought galvanized me into action and I left the social worker standing there while I tore off to get in my car and drive home. It was time to leave him, I'd become stronger through time and it was now or never. My daughter was home with him and I'd be damned if I was going to ever leave her alone with him again.

As I drove home it became very apparent to me that one of the reasons I couldn't leave Greg was because I was weak and afraid. I was afraid of everything. I was afraid of not being able to support my children alone. My wages were not enough to support myself let alone a family.

I was afraid of what he would do to me, and to the children if I left him. Fear of the unknown reared its ugly head for just a second on that drive home but I shoved it to the back of my mind and drove on; my anger spurring me to get to my children as soon as possible.

To sum it all up; I was afraid of failure, I was afraid that my children would suffer, I was afraid of poverty, I was afraid of everything. Fear can really throw you a curve. When it becomes firmly entrenched in your mind it prevents you from doing what you have to do to survive, it can also prevent you from thinking clearly so you can make informed and good decisions.

Greg had effectively isolated me for so long I was unable to make any decisions. If I did make any I knew I could never carry them out as long as I stayed with that sadistic monster. This act helped me to see; 'those days of being afraid were finally over.' I wasn't afraid to confront him, I was madder than a hornet, today it would end.

. I was torn between my concern for the child he had hurt and my elation at finally having a way out. I could use this to divorce him and escape. I felt strong and empowered, I thought I could see the light at the end of the tunnel.

I figured he would be so embarrassed when the news of his newest atrocity got out that he would no longer fight me and let me go. Boy was I wrong! Again!

I did not have the foresight at that time to be able to see all that could happen when I told Greg I wanted a divorce. The church taught that their members couldn't get a divorce unless there was an act of adultery or fornication. They did not give abused spouses the help or encouragement they needed because that was not grounds in their eyes for divorce. You stay with the abuser and you work it out unless he cheats on you.

First you had to prove to the elders of the church that an act of adultery had happened. Even then they wanted you to forgive the mate who had 'strayed.' I didn't really care what the elders said or thought. They did not help me and I cared nothing for them.

Unfortunately one of the only ways I could break it off with Greg was to try to enlist the aid of the elders. Later, when I told them of the charges against Greg and that I wanted away from him once and for all, they again gave me no help. Without proof of adultery, I was well and truly stuck in that marriage, at least in their eyes.

These men of power in the congregation didn't even try to talk to my children. They had sworn to their 'god' they would watch over and protect their flock. All they were was a handful of untrained and emotionally unavailable men.

All they ever accomplished by their not taking my story seriously; was to encourage Greg to beat me even worse; they didn't believe me, even with the proof of bruises; he knew that and used it to his advantage.

As I drove up the driveway to our house I felt a myriad of emotions racing through me, they cut paths through my mind and my heart confusing me and elating me all at the same time. Anger of course was at the forefront, but I also felt concern for my relative who had been hurt, fear at what Greg would do when I got home, fear for my daughter, but deep in the back of all these negative and counter productive emotions was hope.

I parked my car in the garage and saw Greg was outside like he had been waiting for me. He always wore a permanently angry look on his face, today he had that face on, but along with the hatred; fear shone from his eyes. I knew that because I saw the look of fear in my eyes; every single day of my relationship with Greg.

I could see the effort he was making trying to school his features into a look of concern. It was almost funny and I would have laughed if I hadn't been so afraid.

Don't get me wrong I was stronger than I'd ever been before. What he had done to my relative gave me the backbone to do what I needed to do, but yes, I was afraid. I was shaking from it, but I stood my ground waiting for him to approach me.

With his concerned façade firmly in place, or so he thought, he walked slowly up to me and asked me, "Why are you home early? Is everything alright?" He then grew silent watching me closely.

His about face from anger to concern put me immediately on my guard. 'He knows that I found out today what he has been up to." I reasoned out quickly in my mind.

In the past when he had shown some kind of concern for me I actually would believe him, those days were gone forever.

"Yes, actually something did happen today, I was visited by a woman from 'Child Protective Services.'"

I grew silent then and waited to see his reaction.

"Really, and what did she have to say to you?" he asked menacingly.

I heard this inflection in his tone and froze. I had to weigh my words very carefully in order to be able to get my children and get the hell out of this maniac's life.

I decided, diplomacy aside, I would use the direct approach. So with a bravado I really didn't feel I told him, "She told me that you were being accused of doing something horrendous to a child, is it true Greg? Did you do what she said?"

He stood face to face with me, his eyes boring into mine and then without any warning his hand shot out and he grabbed me by the throat. He tried to squeeze but he didn't have a good enough grip and I wiggled out of his grasp.

Free of his death grip I ran for the house to find the children. I locked the door behind me and began to scream for the kids. I heard them answer me from the main bathroom where they had locked themselves in. As they heard my voice they opened the door and rushed into my arms.

I don't know what Greg had done to make them seek refuge in a locked bathroom I didn't have the time to quiz them on their reasons, we had to leave. I wasn't sure how I would pull it off but I would get them out of that house and away from the monster if I had to die trying.

I could hear Greg trying to get in the door and knew he would accomplish it soon and get inside. Raw panic engulfed me, I had to do something, but I for the life of me didn't know what.

Greg was through the door now and I heard him approaching me down the long hallway. I made the kids go back into the bathroom and told them to 'lock the door and no matter what, they were not to open the door to anyone but me,' I made them promise and then locked and shut the door.

"What the hell do you think you're going to do?" He taunted me, his face back to his normal hatred and evil.

"What do you think you're going to do?" I asked him throwing his own question back in his face.

My words were like throwing gasoline on a fire and with a loud roar he attacked, grabbing my hair like he so loved to do, he proceeded to pull me across the hardwood floors towards our bedroom.

He already reeked of alcohol even though it was barely noon and in a drunken condition he was much more dangerous. I was afraid, yes, more afraid than I'd been in a long time but like I said earlier; he had gone too far, and I had snapped. No more would I allow him to hurt me or the children.

For the first time I fought back, I kicked and punched at his body knowing I was small and much weaker than him but I would not stop. My arms and legs were kicking and spinning without letup trying to get loose from his grasp. I actually managed to land quite a few blows and he had to let go of me.

I could have run out of the house to freedom right then and there but in the background I could hear the kids calling for me in scared little voices. This was a first for him and for me. I would not cower anymore and hide behind lies and violence. I was going to stay and fight and if I could do something to end this evil mans life then do be it.

I quickly jumped to my feet and faced him, nose to nose like two cowboys staring each other down. Neither of us moved, I could hear his jagged breathing and knew he was for once; unsure of what to do next.

He was showing some fear and seeing this I felt elated. It was intoxicating, the tables were slowly turning, and I was going to try to take advantage of that fact. He was on guard and confused, I wasn't running or crying I was standing my ground and meeting him eye to eye.

That's when I realized that these monsters who abuse women and children are spineless, weaklings who have to prey on those weaker than themselves to bolster their own egos. Sick but true, how do you combat that type of person? I don't know; all I can tell you is that when I stood strong in front of him, he was unable to figure out what to do next.

When you get to the point where you have no choice but to leave, when you tell your mate and then see that look in their eyes; let it empower you. Any confusion or fear that you see, act immediately, don't antagonize, but let you're newly forming self assurance blossom, you will think much clearer and see not just one part of the problem but the whole problem.

I knew without a shadow of a doubt; that he would eventually resort back to violence. As soon as he figured out that no matter what I was doing he could still brutalize me physically all hell would break loose.

I took advantage of his momentary confusion to walk to the door. I didn't run I knew that might spark him into action quicker than if I walked 'confidently,' to the door. Yet, as soon as my hand began to turn the doorknob, I heard him coming for me.

I was lucky that day; I was quicker than him, through the years he'd grown quite out of shape and I on the other hand, because of my hard physical labor, was in excellent shape.

I threw the door open and dashed out just as he reached for my hair. I made it to the front yard and thankfully, the neighbors were all outside, working in their yards, each house on either side of me had enough 'witnesses,' that Greg knew he had lost that round.

He growled at me, "this isn't over, I'll be back."

I looked at him square in the eye and with a strength I didn't knew I possessed I responded to his taunt with; "no, you won't, your things will be in the garage, I am filing for divorce. Goodbye Greg."

He backed away from me, and seeing all the neighbors out he said nothing in return; walked to his truck and left.

CHAPTER 11

I may have gotten a reprieve that day but it was short lived. I did exactly as I told Greg I would; I packed all of his belongings and half of everything in the house and put it in the garage. From the silverware in the kitchen drawer to the pillows on the bed; I gave him half. I made sure I had witnesses and documentation for when I began the divorce procedure.

Material things weren't as important to me as my life and the life of my family. So I happily gave up some physical things to reach my goal of eventually having a peaceful household.

What I didn't count on was that he may try to force his way back into the house. I had witnesses to him leaving angry. But, he was a stupid and ignorant man. Instead of doing what I was doing; getting a lawyer and doing things the legal way he tried to enlist the aid of the elders in the church.

They called me and wanted to set up a meeting with me to talk. Out of respect for them and the time I had spent in their church, I agreed, but in my heart I would not listen to a word they said. My decision was made and I could not be budged.

When I got to the church, Greg was there also, waiting for me in the parking lot. I knew he would not touch me there, the elders were inside waiting for us and all I had to do was scream and they would be there within seconds.

He threw me a curve; he tried to tell me that he loved me and wanted me back. Inside I was silently laughing, no way, like I said before I was done! Besides I knew he was only saying this so he could honestly tell the elders he had tried to reconcile with me. I wasn't stupid anymore, I didn't care, I felt nothing when I looked at him in the darkness, no fear, no remorse, nothing. It was awesome.

The 'meeting,' went about the way I figured it would. They tried to convince me to forgive Greg and return to him. I told them flat out, "no way." I didn't feel the need to say anything more. I would not justify myself to the men who were instrumental in my having to stay with Greg in the first place.

They tried to pray with us, I thought about other things as they talked to their 'god.' I had never gotten any help from religion and on that day I became; 'an unbeliever.'

I suffered through an hour of being read scriptures, and was glad to get out of there and go home. On the way I felt something I hadn't felt in a long time, hunger pains. I had so much stress in my life I very rarely was hungry. I ate out of necessity to keep up my strength. But food was like cardboard in my mouth.

I headed for the McDonalds and ate a Big Mac Meal. It was manna in my mouth. I bought the kids all food and drove home, more relaxed than I'd been in years.

That night, after we all had gone to bed I heard some noises outside. It sounded like someone was trying to open my window. I looked out and saw Greg's truck in the street and freaked out. I didn't wake the kids; I would deal with this myself, but what to do?

The first though I had is what I acted on; I raced to the phone and called the elders in his church. There was one who lived fairly close and within minutes he was there, convincing Greg to go home.

I'm sure he saved my life that night and I am grateful to him for that. He took me seriously and helped me. But I knew that Greg would just get sneakier so without any thought I packed up some things into the car for the four of us and drove away from the house.

I had no idea what to do next; I hadn't thought this out at all. It was an action spurred on by desperation. But it had to be done, Greg would try to get back into the house and I had no desire to be a sitting duck so as we drove on into the night I began to plan, again.

Even though I didn't enjoy the church meetings I had met a woman there who had actually became a friend of sorts. I loved researching, I didn't care what it was about, I loved to learn; so her and I would find complex bible parables, history, etc, and research it together.

It was to her I turned to for help. At first I parked the car in front of her brick home and just sat quietly, wondering if I was going to make a fool out of myself once again by trusting someone with my secrets.

But you never know until you try. Imputing motives in other people is wrong. There are still myriads of people out there who truly care about their fellow man. Sometimes it is up to us to give them the chance to help. Try it; you just might be surprised.

All three kids were asleep in the back seat of the car. I didn't want to wake them up and was weighing my options when the door to the house opened and out came 'my friend,' Janette.

With a warm smile on her face she came to meet me at the car. She began to say something and must have noticed my face; her warm welcoming smile changed to a questioning one.

I knew that look; I had seen it on the face of the woman who had conducted my home bible study. I didn't say a word; I just sat there, waiting for her rejection. I could see she was weighing her options as to what to say to me so I jumped in and spoke first:

"Janette, I'm so sorry I just dropped in like this, it's late, and I know you must be busy so I will just go..."

"Don't be ridiculous!" She interrupted. Noticing the sleeping children in the backseat she offered to help me carry them in and settle them down so we could visit. She said all this so matter of factly I followed her meekly as we got the children into the house.

After we got the three sleepy kids settled in we retreated into her kitchen where she was brewing a hot pot of coffee. It smelled sooo good, I hadn't had any caffeine for a couple of days, and when I smelled the delicious brew I couldn't wait to get a cup.

Janette knew my pension for coffee and without a word poured us both a steaming mug full. She set the coffee down in front of me and sat down herself, staying silent she waited for me to say something first.

I couldn't get a word out, not one word. The last time I had confided in a 'friend,' was still fresh in my mind so I too sat quietly. The minutes ticked away and by the time we had both finished our coffee she broke first and said, "Are you okay? I've seen the way you look at church, like a scared rabbit just waiting for a vicious wolf to jump out and devour you on the spot. You look as if you need to talk so talk away, I'll listen."

I still wasn't comfortable telling all my secrets but her offer was way too tempting to pass up. I told her everything, the beatings, the way he had to rape me when he was mad, which was all of the time. How he forced me to go to the church meetings in order to make sure he looked like the good and attentive husband and when I didn't want to go, how he would beat me making sure the bruises didn't show.

I must have talked for an hour when she put her hand up and said to me, "oh my god, why haven't you told anyone about this? You could be killed; your family could be killed. We have to get you help!"

I wanted so badly to believe she could help me. I explained how I was treated when I approached the elders of the church with my story. I also told her about my experience with my bible teacher, how I had confided in her and she had broke my confidence.

I explained about my doctor turning his back on me and how the police were no help either.

As she sat quietly listening to this part of my story she began to turn red. At first I thought she may be mad because I was saying negative things about her friends in the church, but that wasn't the case at all.

"Are you telling me you went for help and received none? Who could deny help to a woman and her children in such a horrible situation? You all will stay with me and we won't tell anybody where you are until you are ready to be found. In the meantime you can gather your wits about you and do what you need to do to get help."

I can only say I was flabbergasted, this couldn't be happening to me. She believed me and wanted to help. I broke down then and cried for the first time in months, I hadn't cried through the telling of my story to this great friend. But when she showed me the kindness I craved so badly I broke down. I cried for all of the years I was told I was a good for nothing nobody, a whore who had no purpose in life.

I knew deep down that I wasn't a stupid idiot like he loved to say. I was a good mother and person and I would do as she said, I'd rest here in her home until I had the strength and the commitment I'd need to file for a divorce.

I would not be wishy-washy anymore. I'd spent the last years of my marriage being spineless; I'd make decisions and then go back on them because of my fear and weakness. It was time for me to put my family and everyone else who loved me first in my life.

CHAPTER 12

The next week was wonderful, Janette was true to her word, she told no one. The kids seemed to bloom in this stress free atmosphere. They laughed and played again instead of quietly watching the television or just sitting in their rooms trying to be invisible and not catch the attention of their father.

"What had I done to them?" I asked myself as I watched the transformation in my three kids. 'How Could I have let them be put through the hell their father had heaped on them? What was I thinking?' I berated myself over and over again.

During that one week of paradise I made the decisions I needed to make for our future. Sadly one week was all I got, somehow Greg found out where I was staying.

He showed up one night, drunk on his ass and yelling my name from the street. His face reflected in the street lamps revealed a demon, raging and hateful, his desire for revenge stamped on his face.

I hid inside of the house, the doors and windows were all locked, that was a habit I have never been able to break. To this day my doors are locked, I don't like surprises.

He didn't care that the front door was locked; his anger was to the point where he would not be denied entry into my once safe refuge.

Janette wasn't home, she had gone to one of the church meetings, Greg must have known this, whether he had been stalking me or not, I didn't know, but I was sure that I would never put down my guard again, that was a vital lesson for me; one you all should take very seriously.

These meetings were usually two hours long, he knew he would have more than enough time to do whatever he was planning. I was reasoning this all out in my head when I heard him begin to kick at the front door.

Over and over again without letup he kicked, like drums at a funeral, 'you're dead, you're dead,' they seemed to say, like a mantra, shouting my doom.

"Shut up, shut up," I told myself quietly, my imagination was beginning to spin out of control with the old me, I was no longer that person; Janette had helped me to see this fact during the week I'd spent in her company.

She knew I had my belly full of my husband's religious ramblings. It was a mans world and I was to be in submission to them, I think not! This intelligent and kind woman used not the scriptures to reason with me; but common sense and life's stories.

She convinced me it was up to me to take the first step to helping myself. That I'd done, I removed my family from harms way. Greg showing up like that was a set back but a temporary one, I had to step up to the plate and do what's right, and that's exactly what I did.

Rounding up the kids I took them to a playhouse situated in Janette's backyard. After getting their promise they would stay quiet, I went back into the house.

Greg was still beating away at the door; it looked as if the hinges were beginning to weaken; so I grabbed the phone to call the police. As I was explaining to the operator my problem Greg's blows abruptly came to a halt.

Hanging up the phone I put my ear to the door; I could hear voices outside, I didn't recognize one of the male voices but I could hear my husband's voice loud and clear. "Get out of here now before I make you leave!" I heard him yelling.

A strange male voice responded back to Greg in a calm tone, "Come on man, what you're doing is wrong, I know the woman who lives here, she's my friend, and I must insist you leave now or I'll have to call the police."

I didn't hear Greg respond to the man's plea, what I heard was a scuffle ensuing outside. I couldn't get myself to open the door right away but the fact a stranger was out there fighting Greg, for me, propelled me into action and I threw open the door, ready to do battle.

Just as I opened the door I saw a police car pull up Feeling a great rush of relief, I froze, hoping Greg wouldn't see me until the police could approach him first. I hoped they could be a buffer and he would calm down long enough for them to reason with him.

I turned my eyes away from the cop car to see what was happening; what I saw almost made me laugh out loud. Greg was no longer yelling, he must have seen the police car pull up, but he was caught in a great big bear hug by Janette's burly neighbor.

Greg has always had an eerie way with people. He was excellent at convincing them that a lie was the truth. He's the best I've ever seen. When he worked his evil manipulation it's close to impossible to put your finger on what's going on. He actually seems to make sense even though alarms are going off in your head.

He worked this magic of his on the cop and somehow convinced him I was a nut. I overheard him telling the policeman, 'I was mentally unstable and had kidnapped his children.' I couldn't believe my ears, I shouldn't have been so shocked, but I'd never been able to get used to his constant barrage of lies.

Watching Greg trying to manipulate the policeman made me so mad I felt as if I would explode with the sheer force of the emotion. This last week had taught me to be patient and smart, I had to wait for the right time to speak. Silence is golden, that is so true in many cases.

I held my tongue and waited. After Greg had his say the policeman turned to me and asked for my side of the story. I was grateful for this and told him in as few words as possible why I was staying with Janette, and why the children were with me.

Although he looked at me with skepticism, he told Greg to go home and use the legal system to fight his battles. His advice to me was the same. Although he told me, 'you can't just take children away from their father,' he also said, "Go inside, your husband will go home and in the morning I suggest you get legal help."

It dawned on me after watching my own husband, the father of my children, tell a person of authority I was nuts that Greg wasn't only a monster he was evil. Every single thought that went through that man's mind was bent on new ways to hurt and torment me.

He repulsed and yes, frightened me both. This time my fear would be a healthy fear. It would help to protect me by keeping me on my guard, and it would also help me stay focused. This healthy type of fear can be a life saver.

I may have lost that round, but so did Greg. We had a stale mate; the policeman didn't side with either one of us. He had to go home and I went to gather the kids out of the back yard, with all three in tow I went back into the house, making sure to lock the doors behind me.

CHAPTER 13

I was determined to get my little family back into their own home and into some semblance of a normal life. I knew at this point that when the time came and I completely escaped from Greg; he wouldn't just go away. Like I said before; abusers are like a malignant cancer, they never just go away.

Too bad for me he was the sperm donor for my children, I would have to deal with him for at least the next sixteen years, since our youngest was only two years old. There are things for all of you to remember if you have a situation similar to mine;

Never, never, meet your ex-mate alone, I can't state this strongly enough. When I finally returned to my own home, I found in some papers he had left behind; a brand new policy on my life. You can come to your own conclusions, as far as I was concerned he was going to keep trying to get me alone and eventually succeed in killing me.

Greg returned to our house that night and according to my long time neighbors and good friends, he began to board up the windows to our two-car garage. He was making enough noise to attract their attention so they watched for a while, just long enough to make sure I wasn't home.

They suspected what an abusive person Greg was, so after assuring themselves the children and I were not home, they lost interest in what he was up to and returned to their own activities.

The next morning I received a phone call from one of the elders in the church. Greg was in the hospital. After leaving the previous night, he went home, boarded up the windows on the double car garage, and tried to kill himself by sitting in the cab of his truck and letting the carbon monoxide do its job.

The neighbor, once again hearing suspicious noises coming from the now boarded up garage, went to investigate and found him. He'd packed the truck with all of the kid's favorite toys and all their vital statistics records. If he hadn't been found, he would have been dead within a few more minutes.

When I received that phone call I felt nothing. I wasn't worried in the least. I hoped he still died. There was no way I was going to set foot in that hospital. My hatred for him was such that I'd prayed for him to die. Now that he had come close; all I felt was relief that he would be out of commission for a while.

Once again the elders of the church called me and asked to speak with me. This time I refused. I didn't feel one speck of guilt, and I would not put myself in a position to have guilt heaped onto me. I did nothing wrong, he tried to kill himself, a direct sin against god.

His attempt at self murder should have put him in the back room with those elders, but instead they focused on me. Maybe they did speak to him and I didn't know about it. That is possible, all I know is I would never let him make me feel guilty again.

In my eyes his, 'attempted suicide,' was nothing more than an attention getter. I believed that then and I still believe it to be true today. His grip on me was slipping away, I left, and he could no longer control anything I did.

I need to testify here that I am no expert. I do not have a degree in psychology or anything else. I come to my own conclusions by my life experience. Everything I state I believe to be true, it was in my case. All situations are different, so please remember; this is my story. Many tales of abuse are similar, but it is still impossible to generalize because no two situations are exactly alike. Yet, there is a wealth of information in this book, enough to hopefully help anyone living with abuse.

I want nothing more than to be able to instill hope and strength into everyone who reads my story. Empowerment can come from many avenues, friends, family, your own convictions, and strengths; it can also come from those who have lived to tell their own true to life stories.

Keep an open mind; do not immediately dismiss good advice. Think first, analyze the advice, weighing the pros and the cons, and then make an educated decision. Try not to cloud your mind with negative thoughts.

I do not disagree with reconciliation. People can change; whether religious beliefs are instrumental in helping an abuser change or some other source, I applaud anyone who has gone through that type of transformation. It takes guts and fortitude, and most importantly; the ability to be able to be truthful with yourself and honest with others.

Whether you're a man or a woman; abused or an abuser; just be honest with yourself. Life is way too short to be unhappy and completely miserable. Living each and every day with the burden of a self imagined guilt; tears away at the very core of your being, leaving you a shell of your former self.

Living every single day knowing you hurt the people you swore to love must eventually wear away at you also. How can anyone be happy by hurting others?

Abuse affects every single aspect of your life. It also interferes with every single relationship you have. Your work will suffer, your health will suffer, and your family will suffer. Especially the innocents; your children, they look to us for guidance and if we are not emotionally, physically, and spiritually available to them, it is devastating to them.

They are not able to process emotions like adults can. This was so damaging to my children I still get upset when I think of how I hurt them. When there was horrible anger in the house, they suffered emotionally. It ate away at them causing them both to become emotionally unavailable themselves.

I've spent many years trying to make it up to them. How do you do that? There's a book I would love to read. I'm glad to report all of my children have a loving and close relationship with each other and with me.

CHAPTER 14

While Greg was recovering in the hospital; I retained an attorney. He was a good man and I felt comfortable with him.

I knew hiring an attorney was expensive; but I had no choice, I knew Greg would be difficult and I wasn't up to the challenge, I needed the expertise of a lawyer. I would work two or three jobs to pay him if I had to.

My Lawyer, after meeting Greg; became so incensed at the way Greg spoke to me and to him, he told me I didn't have to pay the whole bill, and we would discuss money after the divorce was final.

It was wonderful news. I was at my wits end trying to find a supplemental job, but now I didn't have to worry, at least not right then. When my divorce became final I would worry about the bill then.

Pulling no punches; my attorney informed me that in some cases; like mine, the abusive mate could become even more dangerous. He'd worked on cases where the woman ended up in the emergency room with life threatening injuries caused by their 'spurned' abusive mate.

It would take me two more years and being stalked by him to finally get my divorce.

After he had found me at Jeanette's house I made sure I was always very aware of all of my surroundings. I never left the house to go to the car without first surveying the yard to make sure he wasn't waiting for me.

Even when he was no where to be seen, he always showed up wherever I went. This drove me crazy. I never put down my guard but still; he seemed to be able to know every step I was going to take next.

It was summer time when all this took place. I still worked at a nursery and loved nothing more than to go early, at first light, when there was no one there but me.

It was so peaceful. A creek ran adjacent to the property, and in the morning it bubbled happily, attracting birds of all kinds. It made me happy and calm.

All that came to a crashing halt when one morning after I'd arrived at work, alone, without a soul around, Greg showed up. I worked in a big shed where we would pot up plants, there was an access road running beside where I was working, and this is where I saw Greg.

There was only one way in and one way out. He drove slowly past the entrance to where I was working, he didn't stop, he didn't say a word, he just drove by staring at me.

Like I said there was only one way in and one way out. I knew he had to turn around at the end of the road and come back by the entrance to the shed again. I wasn't going to get trapped inside of that shed so before he could return I ran.

I was alone on thirty acres of land; I was scared to death so I ran even faster. I heard a truck motor before I saw it and my heart sunk. He'd found me, there was no where to hide out in the fields. The office was locked up and I didn't have a key.

Somewhere in the back of my head it dawned on me that the sound of the truck engine was coming from the opposite end of the road, it was one of the workers. An older man; he loved to come to work early also. He didn't do this every morning but man was I glad he decided to today.

I ran towards his truck just as Greg drove around the corner of the shed. There was nothing he could do and he knew it. His look said it all; 'next time,' as he left he smiled at me until he was finally out of sight.

Greg wouldn't leave me alone after that. It was as if my refusal to forgive him was making him spin out of control even more than usual. Everywhere I went with or without the kids he would show up.

He would pick flowers out of my yard and try to give them to me. This also meant nothing to me. He sent me notes begging my forgiveness; he told me his suicide attempt made him realize how important his family really was.

He promised he would never, ever hurt us again. A tune he'd sung many times before. This also meant nothing to me.

"Forgive you?" I threw at him, "no, I will never forgive you. I want a divorce." I couldn't understand why he pleaded so hard. He obviously knew I would not be swayed; it was not too long before I found out the real reason for his begging my forgiveness.

His friends and peers in the church were beginning to notice a change in Greg. He was unable to keep up the façade of being a good Christian forever and that false front had begun to slip.

As a result; he was being questioned by the older men of his church about his behavior. They had called me and asked me once again; to come and talk to them. I had told them 'no,' the last time, but somewhere in the back of my mind I felt they may be able to put a stop to Greg's stalking. So we all met once again.

This time it was different, I was talked to kindly and asked if the kids and I were doing okay. They showed sincere concern for our welfare. They didn't immediately berate me and make me feel as if I were a bad person.

During that meeting a lot of truths came out. Greg confessed to having numerous affairs throughout our marriage. In front of the leaders of the church he asked for my forgiveness.

Once again I told him; 'absolutely not.' He went so far as to get down on his knees in front of me as a 'show,' for our onlookers. I sat cold and silent. I felt nothing but disgust and loathing.

The elders told me that I did not have to forgive Greg, he had committed adultery by his own admission and I had the god given right to divorce him. I was already in the process of divorcing him. They told me it was against god's law to start the divorce without knowing if there had been ground for a scriptural divorce.

I told them, 'I didn't care about 'god's' law, my decision was made.

Once they realized I could not be swayed, they gave in. They did everything they could to intervene between Greg and I that night. I stood my ground and eventually they began to 'council' Greg about his behavior. I believe deep down those men were embarrassed they had denied me help when I needed it the most. They all realized I had been telling the truth and were ashamed.

I tried to forgive them, I felt they were trying to help now, even though I didn't want their help, I still hoped their influence on Greg could control him and he would leave me alone for good.

The result of that meeting was; I was talked into giving Greg joint custody of the kids and I agreed to accept a mere two hundred dollars a month from him for the support of all three of his children.

I knew this amount was petty, but if it meant I was rid of him then that was fine with me. I would just do what I did best and get another job and be the one to support the kids myself. I can honestly say; this was very self gratifying. I felt as if I was worth something when I was the sole provider of my children.

Greg finally gave up stalking me and turned his attentions to getting back in the good graces of the church. Thank goodness! Yet; he continued to torment me in different little ways.

He refused to sign the divorce papers, over and over again. Finally my lawyer forced him legally to undergo psychiatric evaluation; the results were instrumental in my finally gaining my freedom.

I suppose I could play the blame game, but I did what the church leaders wanted and I gave joint custody to Greg; along with the ridiculously low child support. I made the decision to do this, they gave their advice; unfortunately I took it. My fault!

It was a good thing I had hired a very good lawyer. He made sure I received physical custody of the kids. He also helped me to see when I was given bad advice and then gave me the legal advice I truly needed. Not some advice from a bunch of church leaders. They are not lawyers nor do they read hearts.

CHAPTER 15

All victims of abuse can benefit from some type of therapy. I'm not saying all of you need to go to a psychiatrist, not at all. What I'm saying is anyone who is being or has been abused needs something to help them focus and put things back into perspective.

My forethought and vision became muddy due to the abuse I'd suffered for so many years. Therapy can help you to put it all back into place so you can make the right decisions for yourself and your family.

My husband forced me to go to the elders of his church for 'counseling,' I will be honest and say they never once accused me of being a bad person. They may have given me the wrong advice as far as I'm concerned, but their goal was to preserve the marriage.

There are many avenues for victims of abuse and I believe the church could be one of those avenues. Just because I had a bad experience doesn't mean there aren't many, many religious leaders who care and want nothing more than to help. Along with state and local authorities; there are professional people out there who will come to your aid.

You can't help yourself or your family until you heal your mind. A master manipulator such as Greg; is hard to fight. They actually begin to make sense. They can turn black to white and night to day with just a word. The elders were no match for Greg. They were nice but untrained and naïve. Their actions told me that.

I'd been associated with the church for quite a few years. During those years I only went through the motions of being a believer, I did this to avoid the beatings I would get if I didn't want to go to the meetings with him. Besides it didn't hurt me to go to their meetings. They were very educational and sometimes interesting.

I loved to study and I used those times at the meetings to listen and then go do my own research on whatever subject they had been talking about. It was in this way I grew in my knowledge of the scriptures and what they 'meant.' I would go to the local library and research using; secular history, and other non-secular research materials.

All of my research was interesting and because of what learned I call myself an unbeliever. I didn't come to this conclusion lightly, I spent a lot of time and energy on my studies, and I came to this conclusion, not out of ignorance of the bible but out of knowledge.

I also managed to make some wonderful friendships at the meetings. Jeanette for one, by her steadfastness as a friend she just may have saved my life and the life of my children.

After my divorce was finalized I made the decision to cut off all ties with religions, period. I'd been from church to church looking for an answer to all my questions, what I found out was it was my own strength that would ultimately save me.

The friends I'd made in the church stood by my decision and they are still true friends to me today. Many of the parishioners chose to shun me for my decision. They practiced disfellowshipping for unrepentant sinners. I wasn't disfellowshipped from the church; I simply walked away. But there were still those who chose to put me in a category of sinner, and are still shunning me today.

Maybe I could have told all those people who refused to associate with me the truth about my life, but what would that prove? I wasn't proud of it and had no desire to share my story with anyone.

If they chose to shun me without the facts; that was okay with me, they helped me to be able to recognize a true friend from a false one. I learned to pick and chose my friends carefully after that. I'm pleased to say I have chosen wisely, I have so many good and close friends today; that I feel I can say I am 'blessed.'

If you're reading this and you are a victim of some type of abuse, please, please, get the help you so badly need to save yourself; before it is too late. If conventional therapies are not what you feel is best for you, find something else.

I cannot stress this enough; whatever you feel will work for you, do it. Don't hesitate; don't let your brain overwhelm your thoughts with negative ones. 'It won't work, I'm no good, nobody wants to help me, etc…" That type of poisonous thinking kept me from escaping Greg sooner.

As I result I spent more years under his tyranny than I had to. Once again; get help, get it now. Don't put it off until you feel you will be stronger, don't use any lame excuses because; that is exactly what they are.

Abuse is a life and death situation. Don't force your loved ones to have to view you in a coffin. Don't put them through the trauma of your violent and unnecessary death. Or maybe you won't die, sure that is a possibility also, maybe you'll just be maimed or disfigured for the rest of your life.

Instead of you being killed; maybe it will be your children who have to be the ones viewed by their loved ones in their caskets. Picture that and then ask yourself; 'Is this what I want my family or myself to come to?"

Greg was still a thorn in my side for many months I still had the kids in common with him and I had to contend with that. I kept to the court ordered visitations even though I didn't collect much in the way of child support. Instead of reasoning out; child support is to support his children. He withheld it to punish me.

I just worked more and harder. I didn't have the energy to fight him anymore. I took what he gave me and took care of my children myself.

Even though we were divorced and I had physical custody of the kids Greg decided to try one more time to 'reconcile.' I know his goal was to put a stop to his child support payments, I was no dummy anymore.

I'd come home from work early after receiving a phone call my daughter was sick at school. When I arrived home I saw Greg's truck in the street in front of the house but he was no where to be seen.

'Oh crap,' I thought, 'what now?' Telling my daughter to stay put in the car I approached the house slowly, on my guard. The door to the house was still locked, so I opened it wide and tried to see inside without actually entering. I didn't want to get myself trapped by Greg. I'd learned a lot in the months following my escape from him. I was cautious and quiet.

I couldn't see Greg anywhere but what did catch my eye was a bouquet of flowers on my kitchen countertop. There was a note attached and in it Greg asked me to return to him. It wasn't the note or the flowers that set me to running; it was that silent alarm in a mother's head that goes off when danger is near.

The house had all new locks; that was the first thing I'd done after returning home. 'He didn't have a key,' I puzzled out to myself as I sprinted outside to check on my daughter who was still waiting in the car.

What I saw made my blood freeze. Greg was bent over and leaning into the car attempting to remove my daughter's seatbelt. 'Oh hell no,' I fumed to myself as I drew close to the car. This would not happen ever again, not without a fight.

There was a baseball bat leaning against the garage wall and this is what I picked up and carried with me to the car. I was not afraid and I was ready to do whatever was necessary to keep Greg from taking her from me.

He must have heard me approach for he jumped up guiltily and smiled. There was no way I would be put off my guard, I held the bat ready to swing and waited without a word for him to make the first move.

I would swing that bat and I would take his head off if I could. I absolutely wouldn't hesitate, not then and not now. I would protect my family from harm and never stop.

He was sizing me up; when he saw I was not going to back down he hesitated, just for a second. But it was long enough for me to gain the confidence I needed and I swung my body around until it blocked the open door to my daughter.

With my bat at the ready I stood my ground, he actually took a step backwards, then another one and then another. Neither of us said a word then as he reversed his actions and took a step towards me a car drove up the driveway.

It was my brother and boy was he a sight for sore eyes. As he exited his car he ran over to me and took the bat from my shaking hands. I would have done whatever was necessary at that point, thank goodness my brother showed up and I didn't have to.

Greg, like the coward he was, seeing he was outnumbered ran to his car and with a squeal of his car wheels left.

This was the first time one of my family had actually witnessed Greg in action. This was a milestone for me that day. I had the eye witness I needed from my family. Greg knew it also.

From that day on Greg continued to harass me, calling me names, and telling the kids I was worthless. But that was okay, words don't mean a thing if their used to hurt. Not a thing.

It would still take months for Greg to get it through his thick skull that I wouldn't ever return to him. Never! I'd gotten a taste of freedom and it tasted sweet.

I use the term freedom because as anyone who has lived in an abusive relationship knows; living the life of abuse is akin to being in prison. It's just like being put into solitary confinement; you have no life, no friends, and no hope.

I felt free. Free to do what I wanted without worrying about what was going to happen to me if I didn't do everything his way. This feeling of freedom didn't come easily. I had to work very hard, every single day,

By the time you gain your freedom you begin to take on a 'new personality,' actually it's your original self, but because it had been imprisoned for so many years it was difficult to remember exactly who I was.

I wasn't a whore or a slut; I never was a bad person or a bad mother. I'd drifted away from what being a mother was all about because of my abuse; but today I know; I am nothing like Greg said.

Oh sure, I still told myself I was worthless and I actually let this idea prevent me from blossoming after my divorce. There were things I thought I wanted to accomplish but was too afraid to try them. I still was beaten down to a certain extent and that was what I would fight the rest of my life.

Just the fact I finished this work shows; I am well and good on the road to healing. It's been years and it still affects me today, when my present husband who is the most wonderful man in the world points out something I did incorrectly, I crumble mentally and tell myself, I'm a failure.

When he sees this he gives me the truth and encouragement I need to carry on. Women like us will never completely heal. There will be emotional baggage for the rest of our lives.

I encourage you to find good and balanced friends and relationships and shed the past. It's just that; the past. It's dead and buried, rise up, and become whoever you want to be.

An author, a doctor, a psychiatrist, or just a stay at home mom, you can do it, I know, this book is proof it's possible.

CHAPTER 16

I may have been able to heal and gain my freedom from Greg's oppression but what about my children? How are they today? Did their experience with Greg affect their adult lives?

Next; are a couple of the questions my daughter will attempt to answer in this chapter? She's the oldest and the child who got the brunt of Greg's insane parenting. I hope to tell her complete story at another time. Today I will ask her key questions to try to draw her out of her shell, which, yes, she still lives in today, and not only help you, the reader; but also help her at the same time.

This chapter is for all the children who lived the nightmare of an abusive and dysfunctional childhood. I hope with all my heart this will help relieve the guilt and confusion that may have followed you through your life.

No matter how the answer makes you feel, we; as parents; have a lot to answer for and we have to help our children adjust as they grow; that is our responsibility as parents, I'm sure you will agree with this if you are a parent like me whose kids suffered right alongside of you during whatever abuse you suffered from.

I'm glad to write the answers my daughter had for me; even though some of those answers were a direct result of my own actions, and they were like an arrow piercing my heart, I needed to hear what she had to say and so do you.

The first question I asked her was this: 'How has the abuse you suffered as a child affected you in your adult life.' I purposely made this question all encompassing in order to draw out anything and everything she wanted to say.

"I first noticed my family was different when I was around five years old. The kids I played with were happy and always doing things with their families. Their parents were always together, unlike my own family where no one smiled and no one seemed to care.

As early as I can remember my father took us to church, at least three times a week. I didn't enjoy those meetings. Besides the usual boredom all kids suffer when they have to sit in an adults world and 'listen,' to a boring speech, the people in the church made me very uncomfortable.

They had a way of making me feel as if everything I did was wrong, we had to sit quietly because every single thing we did was scrutinized, it seemed as if anything we might say was taken out of context and used by my father and other adults in the church to get me in trouble.

The result of this type of emotional treatment is; I am a very untrusting person today. I set very high standards for myself and others. When I fail or they fail I feel a deep disappointment that is close to impossible to shake off.

I take every negative thing in my life and blame myself for it. An example of this is; if someone hurts me, I find a reason why it's my fault, even if it's not my fault.

I take criticism better than I take praise or compliments. I don't believe someone is complimenting me because I've done anything right, I think they are just feeling sorry for me.

I'm very independent and I don't rely on anyone to do anything for me. I have learned to forge my own path, and to accept any consequences that come my way, good or bad. I tend to refuse any offer of help, I worry that if I accept help from anyone I'm weak.

I have very low self esteem, I know this because as I stated before; I blame myself for everything that goes wrong in my life. It's made me independent but my independence is extreme and unbalanced.

I don't feel the need for a man to take charge of me. I am married and I love my husband, he is not abusive and loves me to death. But I still blame myself for everything, if I don't get dinner on time; I blame myself and beat the living hell out of myself.

My mind actually tells me I'm to blame, for what? I don't know half the time, but it's still my fault. This is a direct result of my childhood.

I'd much rather pay my own way than accept, 'charity,' even if it's not charity, I imagine it is; and then beat myself up. For example; if someone offered to give me some nice clothes that were too small for them I wouldn't accept it. I know now they just wanted to find a home for some good clothes, but I thought otherwise.

My father would take us to the homes of his friends in the church and beg. He would actually show up at their houses with us in tow at dinner time. Do you know how embarrassing and traumatizing that is for a child?

He would ask them for food and clothing for us. I was humiliated and to this day have a hard time accepting help or anything else from anyone. I always hoped my mother would tell him, 'no, we will not go to your friend's house and beg,' but she didn't.

I now know it was because he would beat her for her insolence.

My father constantly embarrassed me in public. I found myself wishing I could become invisible. He would flirt with waitresses in restaurants; actually he flirted with any woman he was around, even with my mom right there with him. He was loud and obnoxious, I hated it when he would announce we were going to go eat or anyplace else that was public. Where other children I knew loved to be with their parents I feared it.

To sum up my answer to your question; growing up in a violent and religious household has affected every single thing in my life. It's affected the way I treat people around me, my husband, my brothers, and even my own daughter.

I tend to be weak around her, I slack on discipline because of the way my father made me feel when he would, 'discipline,' me. It's very hard to explain but when you are little and being told you've done something wrong and you sincerely don't know why and are spanked and put in 'timeout,' it does something to you inside.

I didn't know why my emotions were so raw at the time. I felt; stupid, unloved, and all alone.

My mother was there for me to a certain extend but she had to contend with her own abuse so I retreated inside of myself and barely spoke to anyone. I figured if I kept quiet I wouldn't be blamed for everything.

With a father like mine, this didn't work. He still blamed me for things I had no idea of. My mind was a constant whirlwind of confusion mixed with depression. When you are a little girl and 'know' no one loves you its devastating.

When I would go to school I never spoke. The teacher's were nice and they tried to figure me out but I would not let them in. There were kids at school who I made some type of friendships with but they were all superficial, a necessity so I could fit in with them.

Because of 'our religion' I had to spend every holiday in the school office with the secretary. I was so embarrassed of this, the rest of the class asked me why, but you know; I really didn't know why. My parents tried to explain this to me but all I knew was; I had to sit in full view of the whole school while they ate their cupcakes and had their holiday fun.

My mom tried to ease this for me by coming to the school to pick me up when she knew the parties would begin. When my father found out she was doing this he put a halt to it right away.

"How will they learn to defend their faith if they aren't put in the position to have to?" I heard him ask my mother when he found out she'd gone to pick me up.

"It's embarrassing and hard on them," my mom told him. I heard him slap my mom then, I don't know if I can put into words how it felt to hear that.

I told myself it was all because of me, I was bad and weak. My mommy was being hurt by my daddy because of something I'd done. Out of all the abuse and all the years we lived with that man, this was the hardest thing for me to take.

My insides felt shredded and I didn't know how to feel or what to think anymore. I felt myself retreat back into myself and there is where I stayed for years and years.

2. How does it make you feel to talk about your past?

"I'm okay talking about it. I've never done this before and I'm hoping I can purge some of my past experiences by giving this interview. But, I don't like the fact my talking like this is causing me to examine myself. I don't know if I'm ready for all of the emotions that it's stirring up.

Still; I'd recommend this to all the adults who were abused children. It's good to talk out loud, it's hard, but it feels very uplifting to unburden myself like this. Sure my emotions are coming to the surface as fast as I can speak, but I will deal with them if it means I can shed some of the unwanted weight I've carried with me for so long.

3. I realize there are so many things I can ask you, but that will be the subject of another book, for now; what advice do you have for all the children who have walked in your shoes?

"My advice is this! Whatever abuse you suffered in the past, it was not your fault. Don't allow what has happened in your childhood to affect your decisions as an adult.

The negative thoughts that go along with your dysfunctional past are counter-productive. They will only hold you back from doing whatever you need to; to succeed in your future.

Don't use your past as a crutch or excuse for failure. An honest self assessment is key to good decision making.

If you blame the fact your father beat your mother and abused you also as an excuse for a failed job interview or a reason not to enter into a healthy relationship, then you need help.

Instead; use these 'failures' as a learning tool to better equip yourself for the next job interview or the next relationship. I did and I can honestly say; "I'm beginning to see the truth of my past and am able to tell myself; it was not my fault.

I still cannot allow myself to give into my emotions. I find it difficult to cry, I still have problems opening up to people, but these are things I can work on. So should you. To cry is like a pressure relief valve and is very healthy. Believe me I want to breakdown sometimes but I do not give in to that desire, instead I hold it in.

I want all of you reading this to know I realize this is a dangerous thing; to keep your emotions bottled up. This is my burden; I will work on this for the rest of my life because of the way I was treated by my parents.

My final advise is this: If you are a child and living in a dysfunctional and or an abusive household, tell someone. Your Pastor, other family members who have no idea of what your going through, even the police.

If whoever you tell doesn't believe you, that's okay, move on to the next avenue of help and keep going until you find that one person who will believe you and give you the help you need.

It will happen eventually, hopefully you won't have long to search but if you do keep your negative emotions at bay by telling yourself; 'I've done nothing wrong and I will get help.'

Make this your new mantra, don't become emotionally detached, you will have to live through many upsets, but that one person is out there, your savior, whoever chooses to give you help, let them.

Don't make it difficult by denying their help or playing the blame game. When my mom finally left my father I was the happiest girl in the world. I felt nothing but fear and loathing for too long.

I think it took my mom way too long to leave my dad, but once she had made the decision she became an unmovable anchor. I watched as she got stronger and stronger and began to stand up for what was right.

She wouldn't say she hated my dad or that he was bad or evil, even though he was. She taught me a vital lesson in morality and life by always using what my dad did as a learning tool.

She would explain to me that what he was doing was wrong and then explain why. I respect the fact she didn't try to turn me against him by calling him names or saying he was a horrible person. The result was; I made my own judgments about my father.

I haven't seen him in quite a long time and I want it to stay that way. I now have a wonderful daughter who is happy and safe; I will not allow her to be around my dad. His evil influence will not taint my family in any way. He's gone out of my life forever and I am as happy as I can possibly be.

I hope that I've made a difference in the life of those who read this. I worry every single day about the silent children who are out there right now, living like I did; in hell. I wish I could gather them all together and keep them safe.

Of course that's not practical; all I can do is tell my story and hope I've touched the life of those who have walked in my shoes.

EPILOGUE

I've included some final information that I hope will help all victims of abuse. As you read the statistics I've included I hope you all take it to heart, and use it to escape yourself.

Domestic violence is the dirty, little secret that is a common thread weaved into the fabric of all societies. It does not discriminate against race, religion, culture socioeconomic status, or gender.

However the victim in the majority of domestic violence cases is female.

According to statistics on spousal abuse, one-third to one-half of adult women have been abused by her spouse or significant other.

It is estimated that over half of the attacks on women are perpetrated by someone they know, usually a husband, or a boyfriend. Domestic violence is usually a response by the male in an effort to control, physically, mentally and/or emotionally, his female partner.

The victim of spousal abuse generally lives in fear, intimidation, and humiliation. Her abuser makes her a captive in her own home and in her own life as the abuser exerts power and control over her. Because of his manipulation and her isolation and lack of emotional support, the female becomes dependent on the abuser for everything, including her identity.

Statistics on spousal abuse indicate that once a victim is isolated from her friends and family, the domestic violence becomes more intense.

Types of domestic violence include: physical abuse, verbal abuse, emotional abuse, sexual abuse, and economic deprivation.

Many victims of domestic violence find themselves isolated from family and friends and humiliated by their situation.

It stand to reason that many cases of domestic violence go unreported. Statistics on spousal abuse demonstrate that the majority of women who are victims of abuse do not report these occurrences to either their physician or anyone else.

Some of the injuries are so severe that hospital admission or serious treatment is required. In addition, the vast majority of these incidences are never reported to the police.

Abuse such as verbal and emotional abuse are not considered criminal acts, but these types of abuses can, and many times do, lead to criminal behaviors, such as assault.

The common response to an issue of domestic violence is to wonder why the woman just does not leave the abuser. As with any other relationship, there are many factors that affect a female's decision to stay with her abuser. Some of the most cited reasons that a female stays with an abusive spouse are:

*Fear and Shame
*Lack of resources {financial, support, etc}
*Children
*Feelings of guilt
*Promises of reform by abuser
*Love for her spouse

Spousal abuse is cyclical, and there are distinct phases to spousal abuse. The abuse begins as the male's frustrations and stresses built. According to spousal abuse statistics, more like than not, the female will continue to face abuse as long as she is with the abusive partner regardless of his promises to change.

Spousal abuse goes underreported by female victims, and when the victim seeks medical help only a small percentage of cases are reported as domestic violence cases. Spousal abuse is a persistent, silent epidemic that affects millions of women each year.

DOMESTIC VIOLENCE STATISTICS

Between 1/3 and 1/2 of all adult women are beaten by their husbands or lovers at some time in their lives. 14% of American women acknowledge having been violently abused by a husband or boyfriend.

92% of women who were physically abused by their partners did not discuss these incidents with their physicians; 57% did not discuss the incidents with anyone.

In the U.S., every 9 seconds a woman is physically abused by her husband.

Within the last year, 7% of American women (3.9 million) who are married or living with someone were physically abused, and 37% (20 million) were verbally or emotionally abused by their spouse or partner.

According to the California Department of Justice, 246,315 calls alleging incidents of domestic violence were reported back in 1994.

Two-thirds of attacks on women are committed by someone the victim knows—often a husband or boyfriend.

The level of injury resulting from domestic violence is severe: 218 women presenting at a metropolitan emergency department with injuries due to domestic violence, 28% required admission to the hospital, 13% required major treatment. 40% had previously required medical care for abuse.

42% of murdered women are killed by their intimate male partners. 4,000 women are killed each year because of domestic violence.

Women are more often victims of domestic violence than victims of burglary, muggings, or other physical crime combined.

Domestic violence is repetitive in nature; about 1 in 5 women victimized by their spouses or ex-spouse reported that they had been a victim of a series of at least 3 assaults in the last 6 months.

35% of emergency-room visits by women are for symptoms that may be the result of spousal abuse; as few as 5% of these victims are ever so categorized.

The FBI estimates that a woman is raped every 6 minutes in the U.S. Rape victims range in age from 4 months to 92years.

40% of all rapes occur in the victim's home.

An estimated 70% of men who abuse their female partners also abuse their children. In homes where spousal abuse occurs, children are abused at a rate 1500% higher than the national average.

According to the Bureau of Justice, nearly ½ of the violent crimes against women are not reported to the police.

Women with a disability or a disabling health problem were at greater risk of being abused.

The rate of wife assault for women aged 18 to 24 years is four times the national average.

Twenty-one percent of women abused by a marital partner were assaulted during pregnancy. Forty per cent of these women said the abuse began during pregnancy.

Children witnessed violence against their mothers in almost 40 per cent of cases.

In a majority of violent episodes the abuse of alcohol was a factor.

One-third of women who were assaulted feared for their lives at some point during the abusive relationship.

Eighty-five per cent of women who had been assaulted said they experienced negative emotional effects like anger, fear, becoming less trusting, lowered self-esteem.

Although abusers can come from any background or walk of life, there are some common characteristics that have been found. An abuser often has poor communication skills, wants to control, places blame on other people or factors for the abusive actions, has little control over impulses, and suffers from a low self esteem.

For some reason, many people "overlook" the extremely damaging emotional and psychological abuse. The abuser will say and do things to shame or insult. They will ridicule and mock the victim in private and even in front of others at times. The abuser tells the victim they are ugly, too fat, too skinny, stupid, lazy, etc.

Other mockeries will include things such as saying the victim can not do things correctly, they do not deserve things, no one else would want them, and other insults that fall into this category. This technique, of course, is also used in the abuse of children.

One thing that will often be heard in an abusive relationship is the abuser stating that the victim "made them do it." This, of course, is totally absurd and untrue. Culture is sometimes used as an excuse or justification for abuse in certain situations. The important thing to remember is that there is NO excuse for abuse, so something like "it's the culture in which he/she grew up" is not valid in the least.

Finally:

One very important fact to remember is that abuse is not classified as an argument or disagreement, nor is it an anger management issue. Abuse is the manipulation of control and power that the abuser wants to have over the victim. They control, they manipulate, and they try to intimidate the victim.

While it is rather easy for someone in a non-abusive situation to believe the victim simply has to leave, it is certainly not that simple for the victim. There is a great fear factor, with the realization that leaving could turn the abuser more violent and in some cases deadly when they find out they are no longer in control.

The victim faces not only fear, but things like shame and isolation as well. We need to be careful not to re-victimize the victim by thinking it is as easy as just walking out. Many times imminent financial difficulties are also a factor, and if children are involved, this anxiety increases. These fears are very real to the victim. Leaving an abusive and controlling situation is the most dangerous time for a victim.

Other factors also play a role in a victim's decision to devise a safety plan and leave the situation. If religious beliefs have strong influence on the victim, or divorce is shameful to a family because of those beliefs, the victim will have even more fears of isolation.

Children are always affected when spousal abuse is present. Often the children are themselves abused, but even if not, things such as poor health due to improper nutrition, excessive crying, and irritability in infants sleep disturbances, and problems with digestion, aggressiveness, nightmares, being withdrawn, having low self esteem, ulcers, and headaches could be a problem. These are only a few of the things that can show up in children who witness abuse, whether physical or emotional.

There are some things to remember when dealing with a victim of abuse. First of all, remember that they have been verbally assaulted and might believe the bad things about themselves that they have been hearing. They will be afraid that you will judge them, so be sure to not do that.

It is very important for a victim to be told and to believe that they do not, nor does anyone, deserve to be abused. Convince the victim that help is available, and make sure you know how to assist in finding that help.

What to do if you are a victim of spousal or partner abuse: Know where local shelters are and have a safety plan to remove yourself from the abusive home or situation. Check with local officials if you are about to leave a situation where physical danger is a threat. You can request a police escort. Also find out about protective orders that might be issued for you, but this should not take the place of an escort.

If there is time to make a safety plan and there is no immediate emergency in leaving, there are some factors to consider. Where will you stay? Do you have emergency money at hand? You may want to move things out a little at a time to where you will be staying.

Last but certainly not least, do not be afraid to ask for help. There are many people and organizations that can help make this transition time safer and perhaps even a bit less stressful for you.

NATIONAL CHILD ABUSE STATISTICS

*There are nearly 3 million reports of child abuse made annually

*In 2003, there were 906,000 child abuse convictions

*The rate of child abuse is estimated to be 3 times greater than is reported

*The rate of victimization is 12.3 children pr 1.000 children

*Children ages 0-3 are the most likely to experience abuse. They are victimized at a rate of 16.4 per 1.000

*79% of these children are under 4.

*These statistics are from the Administration for Children & Families of the US Department of Health & Human Services "Child Maltreatment report 2003"

CONSEQUENCES OF CHILD ABUSE IN THE USA

*80% of young adults who had been abused met the diagnostic criteria for at least 1 psychiatric disorder at the age of 21 (including depression, anxiety, eating disorders, & post-traumatic stress disorder)

*Abused children are 25% more likely to experience teen pregnancy

*Abused teens are 3 times less likely to practice safe sex, putting them at greater risk for STDs

*These statistics are from the National clearinghouse on Child Abuse & Neglect Information. Long-term Consequences of child Abuse & Neglect 2005.

THE LINK BETWEEN ABUSE AS A CHILD & FUTURE CRIMINAL BEHAVIOR

*14.4% of all men in prison in the USA were abused as children

*36.7% of all women in prison were abused as children

*Children who experience child abuse & neglect are 59% more likely to be arrested as a juvenile, 28% more likely to be arrested as an adult, and 30% more likely to commit violent crime.

*These statistics are compiled from US department of Justice Reports

THE LINK BETWEEN CHILD ABUSE & SUBSTANCE ABUSE

*Children who have been sexually abused are 2.5 times more likely to develop alcohol abuse

*Children who have been sexually abused are 3.8 times more likely to develop drug addictions

*Nearly 2/3's of the people in treatment for drug abuse reported being abused as children

*These statistics are compiled from the National Institute on Drug abuse 2000 Report & child abuse & Neglect Study by Arthur Becker-Weidman PhD

Sources:

*Centers of Disease control and Prevention and The Federal Administration for Children and Families. The CEC publication: http//www.cdc.gov/mmwr

*Prevent Child Abuse America; Current Trends in Child Abuse Reporting & Fatalities: The 2000 Fifty State Survey

*"Wife Assault: The Findings of National Survey," Juristat, vol.1, no.9, March 1994

*Statistics on Spousal abuse. 13 Oct. 2008. June 9, 2009.

Washington State

We would like to include the state laws and law enforcement agency phone numbers and addresses. If you have access to this information, please contact us by email to sbcc@computrek.org

Washington State Coalition Against Domestic Violence 200 W Street SE, Suite B Tumwater WA 98501 206-352-4029 (800)562-6025 State Hotline

Eastside Domestic Violence Program P.O. Box 6398 Bellevue WA 98008 Business #: 206-562-8840 Hotline/Crisis: 206-746-1940 Toll Free: (800)827-8840

Lummi Victims of Crime 2616 Kwina Road Bellingham WA 98226 Business #: 206-647-6285 Hotline/Crisis: 206-647-6285

Whatcom County Crisis Services 1407 Commercial Bellingham WA 98225 Business #: 206-671-5714 Hotline/Crisis: 206-734-7271 Toll Free: 206-384-1485

Womencare Shelter 2505 Cedarwood Ave. #5 Bellingham WA 98225 Business #: 206-671-8539 Hotline/Crisis: 206-734-3438

YWCA ALIVE Program Box 559 Bremerton WA 98310 Business #: 206-876-1608 Hotline/Crisis: 206-479-1980 Toll Free: (800)562-6025

Human Response Network P.O. Box 337 Chehalis WA 98532 Hotline/Crisis: 206-748-6601 Toll Free: (800)244-7414

Family Support Center 344 N. Main Street Colville WA 99114 Business #: 509-684-3796 Hotline/Crisis: 509-684-6139

Family Resource Center P.O. Box 907 Davenport WA 99122 Business #: 509-725-4357 Hotline/Crisis: 509-725-4357

Domestic Violence/Sexual Assault Program 220 West 4th Ave. Ellensburg WA 98926 Business #: 509-925-9861 Hotline/Crisis: 509-925-4168

SILENT FOR TOO LONG

Snohamish County Center for Battered Women P.O. Box 2086 Everett WA 98203 Business #: 206-259-2827 Hotline/Crisis: 206-252-2873 Toll Free: (800)562-6025

Forks Abuse Program P.O. Box 1775 Forks WA 98331 Business #: 206-374-6411 Hotline/Crisis: 206-374-2273

Fort Lewis Community Services AF2H-PAW-C Bldg 5218 Fort Lewis WA 98433 Business #: 206-967-7166

Volunteers Against Violence P.O. Box 3175 Friday Harbor WA 98520 Toll Free: (800)562-6025

Programs for Peaceful Living 115 East Main St Suite #2 Goldendale WA 98620

Domestic Violence Center of Grays Harbor 2306 Sumner Avenue Hoquiamn WA 98550 Business #: 206-538-0733 Toll Free: (800)562-6025

Domestic Violence Program Box 11 Incheluim WA 99138 Business #: 509-722-3265

Emergency Support Shelter P.O. Box 877 Kelso WA 98626 Business #: 206-425-1176 Hotline/Crisis: 206-636-8471

Columbia Basin Domestic Violence Services 5917 W. Clearwater Kennewick WA 99336 Business #: 509-735-2271 Hotline/Crisis: 509-582-9841

Domestic Abuse Women's Network (D.A.W.N.) P.O. Box 1521 Kent WA 98035 Business #: 206-656-4305 Hotline/Crisis: 206-656-7867 Toll Free: (800)562-6025

CADA South Whidbey P.O. Box 796 Langley WA 98277 Business #: 206-321-4181 Hotline/Crisis: 206-321-4181

Pathways For Women 6027 208 Street SW Lynwood WA 98036 Business #: 206-774-9843

Our Place P.O. Box 1394 Moses Lake WA 98837 Business #: 509-765-1214 Hotline/Crisis: 509-765-1791

Skagit Rape Relief/Battered Women's Services P.O. Box 301 Mt. Vernon WA 98273 Business #: 206-336-9591 Hotline/Crisis: 206-336-2162

Pacific County Crisis Support Network HCR 78 BOX 336 Naselle WA 98638 Business #: 206-484-7191 Hotline/Crisis: (800)435-7276 Toll Free: (800)562-6026

Family Crisis Network P.O. Box 944 Newport WA 99156 Business #: 509-447-2274 Hotline/Crisis: 509-447-LIVE

Citizens Against Domestic Abuse P.O. Box 190 Oak Harbor WA 98277 Business #: 206-675-7781 Hotline/Crisis: 206-675-2232 Toll Free: 206-321-4181

Safeplace: Rape Relief & Women's Shelter Services P.O. Box 1605 Olympia WA 98507 Business #: 206-786-8754 Hotline/Crisis: 206-754-6300

The Support Center P.O. Box 3639 Omak WA 98841 Business #: 509-826-3221 Hotline/Crisis: 509-826-3221

P.A. Sexual Assault/Domestic Violence Umbrella Community Services P.O. Box 1858 Port Angeles WA 98362 Business #: 206-452-3811 Hotline/Crisis: 206-452-HELP

Port Townsend Domestic Violence/Sexual Assault Pr P.O. Box 743 Port Townsend WA 98368 Business #: 206-385-5291 Hotline/Crisis: 206-385-5291

Connections 470-1 Klondike Rd. Republic WA 99166 Business #: 509-775-3307 Hotline/Crisis: 509-775-3132

4137 University Way NE #201 Seattle WA 98105 Business #: 206-547-8191

Abused Deaf Womens Advocacy Services 2366 Eastlake Ave. E. #30 Seattle WA 98102 Business #: 206-726-0093 Toll Free: (800)833-6388

Abused Women's Project of Evergreen Legal Services 401 Second Ave. Suite 401 Seattle WA 98104 Business #: 206-464-5911 Toll Free: (800)342-5806

Broadview Emergency Shelter P.O. Box 31151 Seattle WA 98104 Business #: 206-622-4933 Hotline/Crisis: 206-622-4933

Catherine Booth House P.O. Box 20128 Seattle WA 98102 Business #: 206-324-7271 Hotline/Crisis: 206-324-4943

Center for Prevention of SA/DV 1914 North 34th Suite #105 Seattle WA 98103 Business #: 206-634-1903

Community Advocate Project 2020 Smith Tower Seattle WA 98104 Business #: 206-296-5240

Consejo Counseling and Referral 3808 S. Angeline Seattle WA 98118 Business #: 206-461-4880

Domestic Violence Services P.O. Box 20128 Seattle WA 98102 Business #: 206-932-5341

East Cherry YWCA 2820 East Cherry Seattle WA 98122 Business #: 206-461-8480

Family Violence Project 710 2nd Avenue Seattle WA 98104 Business #: 206-684-7745

King County Women's Program 2020 Smith Tower Seattle WA 98104 Business #: 206-296-5240

New Beginnings P.O. Box 30821 Seattle WA 98103 Business #: 206-783-2848

New Beginnings for Battered Women and Their Children P.O. Box 75125 Seattle WA 98125 Business #: 206-783-4520 Hotline/ Crisis: 206-522-9472

Protection Order Advocacy Program 516 3rd Avenue Suite E 223 Seattle WA 98104 Business #: 206-296-9547

Refugee Womens Alliance 3004 South Alaska Seattle WA 98108 Hotline/Crisis: 206-721-0243

The Salvation Army/Hickman House P.O. Box 20128 Seattle WA 98102 Business #: 206-932-5341 Hotline/Crisis: 206-932-5341

YWCA Downtown Women's Shelter 1118 5th Avenue Seattle WA 98101 Business #: 206-461-4882 Hotline/Crisis: 206-461-4882

Recovery: Aid to Victims of Sexual and Domestic Ab P.O. Box 1132 Shelton WA 98584 Business #: 206-426-5878 Toll Free: (800)562-6025

YWCA Alternatives to Domestic Violence West 829 Broadway Spokane WA 98648 Business #: 509-327-9534 Hotline/Crisis: 509-838-4428

Skamania County Council on Domestic Violence P.O. Box 477 Stevenson WA 98648 Business #: 509-427-4210 Hotline/Crisis: 509-427-4210 Toll Free: (800)562-6025

Lower Valley Crisis Center P.O. Box 93 Sunnyside WA 98944 Business #: 509-837-6689 Hotline/Crisis: 509-837-6689

YWCA Women's Support Shelter 405 Broadway Tacoma WA 98402 Business #: 206-272-4181 Hotline/Crisis: 206-383-2593 Toll Free: (800)562-6025

VOCA—Yakima Indian Nation P.O. Box 151 Toppenish WA 98948 Hotline/Crisis: 509-865-5121

Safe Choice 1115 Esther Street Vancouver WA 98660 Business #: 206-696-0167 Hotline/Crisis: 206-695-0501

YMCA of Walla Walla 213 South First Walla Walla WA 99362 Business #: 509-529-9922 Hotline/Crisis: 509-529-9922

Wenatchee Rape Crisis & Domestic Violence Center P.O. Box 2704 Wenatchee WA 98801 Business #: 509-663-1952 Hotline/Crisis: 509-663-7446

Programs for Peaceful Living P.O. Box 1486 White Salmo WA 98672 Business #: 509-493-2662

YWCA Family Crisis Program 15 North Naches Yakima WA 98901 Business #: 509-248-7796 Hotline/Crisis: 509-248-7796

You can reach The Sounding Board Counseling Center at:
Voice: 614.231.1164
FAX: 614.338.8059